igloobooks

Published in 2017
by Igloo Books Ltd
Cottage Farm
Sywell
NN6 0BJ
www.igloobooks.com

Distributed in association with © G2 Rights Ltd

HUN001 0717
2 4 6 8 10 9 7 5 3 1
ISBN 978-1-78670-874-8

Cover designed by Nicholas Gage
Edited by Richard Davis

Cover images: © tl Trinity Mirror / Mirrorpix / Alamy Stock Photo;
tc ALAN EDWARDS / Alamy Stock Photo; tr Sport In Pictures / Alamy Stock Photo;
c Maxim Kazmin / Alamy Stock Photo; bl PCN Photography / Alamy Stock Photo;
bc ZUMA Press Inc / Alamy Stock Photo; br Neil Leifer / Getty Images
Addtional cover images: © iStock / Getty Images

Printed and manufactured in China

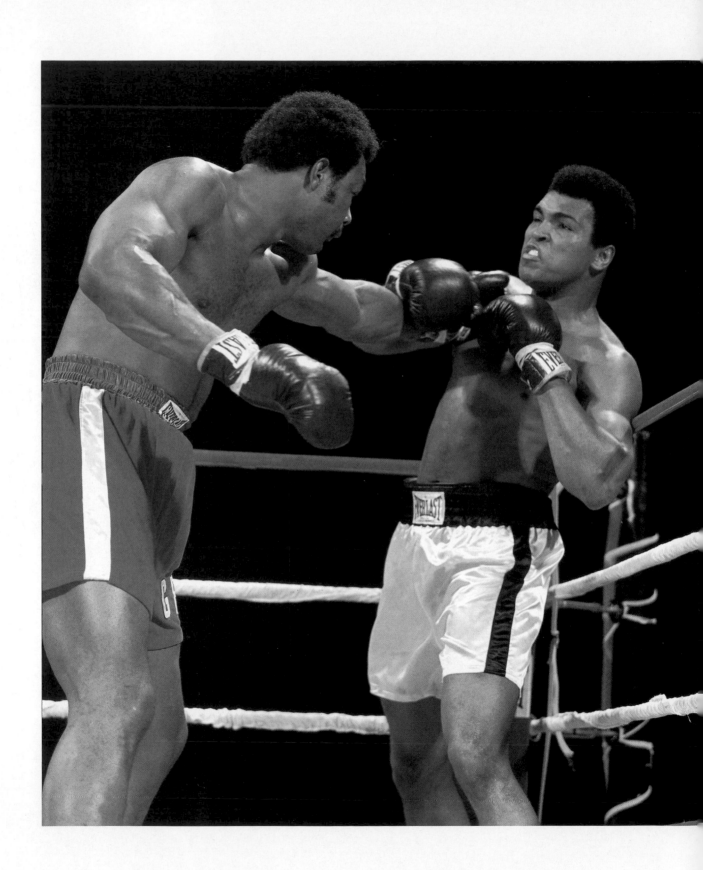

CONTENTS

INTRODUCTION

Lewis Hamilton - page 132

Throughout history, people have pursued sporting prowess, competition and the heights of achievement in a games environment. Friendly sporting contest has been a defining characteristic of what it means to be human and how we relate to each other. Whether through individual battles of will, ability and strength or via team endeavour, we revel in the spectacle and experience of sport.

We start young, both watching and taking part during our school years. For many, these pursuits stay with us, growing and developing as interests as we grow and develop ourselves. They can help to build character, encourage companionship and collaboration and can boost self-esteem and confidence. And a shared sporting passion can of course be a beautiful experience.

Each of us has our favourites. Football, for instance, is the national sport of a few countries, while others favour other games. But "the beautiful game" is representative of the passions that particular sports can inspire in spectators and followers. Fans can and do travel across the globe to support their teams, which can be national or local. Alternatively, millions around the world can watch the same momentous sporting event simultaneously on television at home, or on a bigger screen in a pub, bar or other public place.

Some of the biggest sporting moments in history are featured throughout this book. Such events as the "rumble in the jungle" – Muhammad Ali's epoch-making boxing clash with George Foreman in Kinshasa, in 1974 – for instance. Or England's classic win over Germany in the 1966 World Cup. More recent events, too, are featured, such as Usain Bolt's historic triple-gold at the 2008 Beijing Olympics and golf's "miracle in Medinah" in 2012. There's something for everyone here, with the variety of sports ranging from motor racing, through tennis, to sailing.

Relive those momentous sports occasions, starting with the first modern Olympics in 1896. With a level of detail that will keep ardent sports fans riveted, and glorious, era-defining images, this book is a comprehensive guide to the greatest sporting moments of the last couple of centuries. Read on, to experience those moments once again.

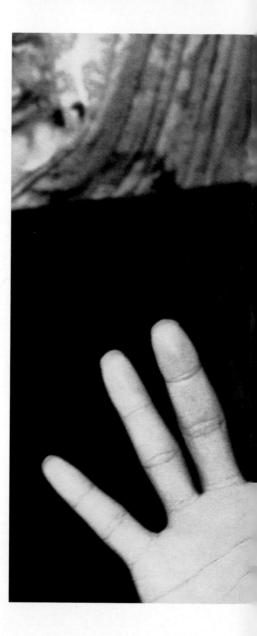

Usain Bolt - page 138

Nick Faldo - page 84

Andy Murray - page 162

Cassius Clay, later to be known as Muhammad Ali, arriving in London for a match with a British opponent, Henry Cooper, in 1963. He is showing his fist and five fingers, representing the number of rounds he will need to knock Cooper out

1896 ATHENS: THE FIRST MODERN OLYMPICS

"I declare the opening of the first international Olympic Games in Athens. Long live the Nation. Long live the Greek people." **King George I**

With an estimated 80,000 spectators filling Athens's newly restored Panathenic stadium and most of the 245 competing athletes arranged by the 14 nations they represented filling the infield, these words, uttered by King George I of Greece, heralded the opening of the Games of the First Olympiad. The date was 6th April, 1896.

The first competition of the inaugural games comprised the opening heats of the 100 metre dash. The American athletes proved outstanding with Frank Lane of Princetown recording a time of 12.2 seconds in that initial round and quarter mile specialists Thomas Burke and Thomas Curtis taking the subsequent two with identical times of 12.0 seconds. The unusual crouched start of these two Bostonians caused much interest with the European audience. Four days later, it would be Burke who took victory in the final by 2 metres from Germany's Fritz Hofmann, once again recording 12.0 seconds.

The honour of becoming the first Olympic Champion since the 369AD victory of Armenian boxer, Prince Varasdates, fell to another Bostonian. Born to a poor Irish-American family, the 27 year old self-educated Harvard freshman and US triple jump champion James Connolly outdistanced popular Frenchman Alexandre Tuffère by over a metre. What should have been a wonderful moment of triumph for the young American was somewhat tainted by the crowds frosty reception to his endeavours. Having dominated the preceding 100 metre heats the Americans were not the flavour of choice for the partisan Greek spectators.

Greek honour was to be restored by the marathon efforts of farmer Spiridon Louis who later revealed that whilst completing his military service a year earlier, as groom to the horses of General Mavromichalis, he had been inspired to compete when shown the finish line of the uncompleted Olympic stadium. To the delight of the 100,000 crowd the diminutive figure of this Greek athlete emerged through the white marble gates of the Panathenic stadium in first place. Rapturous applause followed as Prince George and Crown Prince Constantine ran to his side urging him to the finish where an overjoyed King George stood waiting. Louis's time of 2:58:50 was over seven minutes faster than second placed compatriot Charilaos Vasilakos.

It would be another 108 years before the games would return to Athens in their official form although the enthusiastic Greeks organised an Intercalated (intermediary) Games in 1906. A 1949 commission of the IOC declared that these games were wholly unofficial with the matter remaining closed since.

Crowds walking around the Olympic Stadium in Athens, during the first modern
Olympic Games, in 1896

View of the first modern
Olympic Games in Athens, 1896

The first Olympic medal, a replica
of the obverse, Athens, 1896

1930

THE FIRST WORLD CUP: URUGUAY

There was considerable disappointment within Uruguay over the lack of European entrants for the very first World Cup in 1930. Only thirteen nations competed: four from Europe (France, Belgium, Romania and Yugoslavia), eight from South America (Brazil, Peru, Paraguay, Argentina, Chile, Mexico, Bolivia and Uruguay) and one from North America (the US). There was no need for a qualifying tournament, with the sides being put into four groups, with the winners of each group progressing to the semi-finals.

The host nation left nothing to chance with their preparations, gathering together their squad eight weeks in advance of the competition and shutting them off from the outside world. France and Mexico had the honour of playing the very first match in the World Cup, with France winning 4-1 and Lucien Laurent scoring the very first goal in the tournament. This was to be France's only victory in the 1930 competition, for their group was to be dominated by Argentina, the country from just across the River Plate and potentially the biggest rivals to Uruguay. As such, most Uruguayans who witnessed any of Argentina's matches could usually be relied upon to support the opposition, with the match against the French nearly evolving into a diplomatic incident.

Despite the hostile atmosphere, Argentina took the lead through Luisito Monti and looked to be holding on for a win. As the match headed towards its conclusion, the French rallied and looked capable of scoring an equalizer. With five minutes to go, Brazilian referee Almeida Rego blew for time, but with the Uruguayan crowd storming the pitch and the French protesting, he finally agreed to resume the match in order that it could be completed properly. The Argentineans held on to their lead.

Group 2 was dominated by Yugoslavia, too strong a side for both Bolivia and Brazil, although the Brazilians ran them close, only going down 2-1 after falling two goals behind in the first half. Brazil beat Bolivia 4-0 in what was little more than a consolation after the Yugoslavs had already made sure of their place in the semi-finals.

They were joined by host nation Uruguay from Group 3, who beat both Romania and Peru. The clash between Peru and Romania was notable for the first sending off in a World Cup match, with Mario De Las Casas of Peru receiving his marching orders in front of a crowd of just 300, the lowest figure to have witnessed a World Cup match (qualifying matches notwithstanding).

The fourth and final group was the group that threw up the biggest surprise, for the much fancied Belgian side were eliminated in double quick time.

The victorious national soccer team of Uruguay during the 1930 world cup final.

England batsman Denis Compton hits the winning runs to retain the Ashes for England

Hutton, to Australia's chagrin, decided to play for the draw. While Bedser shut down one end, Bailey held to a defensive line outside the leg stump at the other, conceding just nine runs in six overs. Whether he has yet been forgiven by his opponents for taking seven minutes to bowl one of them is a moot point, but for the second time in the rubber, and in his alternative discipline, he ensured that England retained parity in readiness for a climactic encounter that would hold the nation's attention like no other in recent memory.

Hassett's apparent good fortune in winning his fifth consecutive toss was rendered a chimera by humid conditions at the Oval. England had picked Fred Trueman for the first time that summer and it was an inspired choice, complementing Bedser's accuracy with genuine firepower. They shared seven wickets and Australia had Lindwall (62) to thank for lifting them from 160 for seven to 275. Yet again, Bailey balked Australia; after Hutton made 82 he contributed a dour 64 to ensure a slender lead.

Jim Laker, brought on as early as the sixth over, started Australia's second-innings rot, trapping their captain lbw for 10. He and his Surrey team-mate Tony Lock then worked their way steadily through the order;

despite an exhilarating half century partnership for the seventh wicket between Ron Archer and Alan Davidson, Australia were dismissed for 162. Lock had taken five for 45 and Laker four for 75 and England needed just 132 to bring the Ashes home.

Thanks to Australia's never-say-die bowlers, it took them three and a half hours. The great Lindwall, who finished the rubber with 26 wickets, bowled an 11-over opening spell, and neither he, nor Miller nor Bill Johnston – who bowled unchanged for 23 overs - was easy to get away. Hutton was run out with the score on just 24, but Peter May stayed with Bill Edrich to etch out 64 priceless runs. Edrich was then joined by his "Middlesex twin" Denis Compton who, shortly after three o'clock on 19th August, swung Morris to the boundary at backward square leg.

England's eight-wicket victory sent the crowd of 15,000 into unbridled euphoria. "What a scene here!" enthused commentator Brian Johnston as the ground was flooded with supporters who massed in front of the pavilion to salute their heroes. Staging the last Test of the summer as it habitually does, the Oval has provided the backcloth to many historic moments of which this, surely, was one of cricket's greatest.

1953

BEN HOGAN WINS THE MASTERS GOLF CHAMPIONSHIP

Although it did not happen in the same year, Ben Hogan became the second player ever to achieve a grand slam. The year was 1953 and Hogan was the hot favourite to win the British Open at Carnoustie. The Golf Club hadn't hosted the Open for 16 years and record crowds of 27,000 turned out to see the Irish-American champion play. That he did play was somewhat of a miracle as Hogan had suffered serious injuries in a car crash in 1949 that saw him travel little. But spurred on by his victories in the Masters and the US Open that same season, Hogan was determined to compete. The championship saw him win with a score of 282.

Hogan's Grand Slam was not completed in the same season as the PGA Championship of 1953 was played from 1-7 July while Carnoustie was hosting the British Open from 6-10 July. With a one-day overlap Hogan couldn't play both tournaments and, encouraged by his fellow professionals, he chose the Open. Of the six tournaments that Hogan entered in 1953 he won five – three of them major championships. Arriving just two weeks before the Open, Hogan set out to prepare for his game. He was unaccustomed to the British golf ball which was smaller than the US golf ball at 1.62 inches. He was surprised to find that the smaller ball gave him a much longer strike – more than 15 yards

longer – than its US counterpart and Hogan, renowned for practice, was devilish in his pursuit of perfection. Using a two iron Hogan won the championship. Despite winning he did not return to defend his title the following year and in fact the tournament at Carnoustie was to be his last Open championship.

Hogan had suffered horrific injuries during the car crash of 1949 which left some doubt as to whether the champion golfer would ever walk again never mind kick-start his illustrious career. But undeterred by his fractured pelvis, fractured collar bone and left ankle, chipped rib and terrifying blood clots, Hogan fought back and regained some strength that saw him back on the golf course in 1950 where, although a frail former shadow of himself, his incredible play saw him force a play-off with "Slamming" Sammy Snead which he won. This was to be the start of a career that saw Hogan shine and his years between 1950 and 1953 are hailed by most as his best. The crash had left Hogan with some painful injuries that saw him carefully choose the tournaments he entered and as the best US champion on the golf course he was criticised for not attending more matches. He was a steely, determined man who disliked pomp and circumstance and was a private man who would not be ruled by the politics of the day. So where did it all begin?

Opposite: Ben Hogan tees off during the 1953 Masters Tournament at Augusta National Golf Club in April 1953 in Augusta, Georgia

Ben Hogan signs an autograph during the 1953 Masters Tournament

Hogan was brought up by his mother with his two siblings following the suicide of his father. Born in Dublin, Texas on 13th August 1912, he worked at odd jobs to bring some income into the family home. He was a caddy and later a bank clerk before his destiny took hold and he became a professional golfer during the 1930s. He had moderate success although he also had a great many losses during this time and his career did not resemble that of legends. Today, with the money available to golfing champions, practising the game of golf is a prerequisite, but during the 1930s and 1940s, it was pretty much unheard of. However, Hogan was renowned for the lonely time he spent practising his game and this is what probably turned him into one of golf's sporting legends.

Perhaps marred by a more difficult than usual childhood, Hogan learned to focus, to concentrate and to put in the effort needed to get results. His steely reserve earned him the nickname the "Ice Man" from the Scottish crowds at Carnoustie who were genuinely wowed by his performance but Hogan had a positive outlook on life – despite the Hogan glare which earned him his other nickname "The Hawk" – and quickly established himself with wins, including the US Open, the PGA Championship and numerous US inter-state Open tournaments throughout the 1940s.

Fiercely competitive, Hogan had developed his legendary swing over many years. He was to become the greatest ball striker to have ever played golf having practised for many hours to perfect the swing that left his opponents wilting. It was designed to perform under pressure, and with his non-verbal competition tactic and his seemingly nerveless demeanour, the swing made Hogan a formidable opponent. He gained many critics throughout his career, but mostly for the off-hand comments he made rather than for his game, and he remains to this day one of the most influential golfers to have graced the courses of the US. Hogan died on 25th July 1997 but will be forever remembered as the "perfectionist" of golf.

1958
A GENTLEMEN'S CHAMPIONSHIP

The lacklustre start of the 1958 world championship gave little indication of the drama, controversy and excitement that were to be in store as the year progressed. Nor did it hint at the down-to-the-wire finale or unparalleled sportsmanship that would hand one man the world title and rob the other of his best ever chance of taking motor racing's crown.

The opening round of the competition in Buenos Aires saw little support from many of the major teams. Ferrari sent three of their new Dino 246s for works drivers Mike Hawthorn, Peter Collins and Luigi Musso but Maserati, although well represented with six cars on the grid, were not themselves present, having decided at the end of the previous year to withdraw from racing due to financial difficulties. The only other car present was the Cooper-Climax T43 of Stirling Moss who, with his new Vanwall unready for competition, had been temporarily released from his contract to enable him to take to the start line.

This was to prove a stroke of luck for the Briton and the Cooper team. Electing to drive the full distance without pitting for tyres or fuel, Moss stormed home to victory ahead of Musso and Hawthorn and, in doing so, scored the first ever victory for the Cooper Car Company and the first for a post-war rear-engined car.

As the championship moved to Monaco, the previously dominant Ferraris were once more denied victory as, for a second time, victory went to a Cooper-Climax; this time in the hands of Frenchman Maurice Trintignant. Unfortunately for Moss, he had been forced to retire whilst leading when, after 38 laps, the engine of his new Vanwall failed. Hawthorn immediately took over the

running in the Ferrari but he too suffered mechanical difficulties with a broken fuel pump and was back in his garage just 10 laps later.

Things went considerably better for Moss at the third round held at Zandvoort in the Netherlands. Although out-qualified by his Vanwall team mate, Stuart Lewis-Evans, Moss led from the first corner to the finish line to take an unquestionable victory in complete style. With the BRMs of Harry Schell and Jean Behra taking second and third and a Cooper-Climax driven by Roy Salvadori securing fourth, it was another dry weekend for Ferrari; their best placed machine being that of Hawthorn back in fifth.

The Belgian Grand Prix was another success story for the Vanwall team. This time it was Tony Brooks who took victory honours with Lewis-Evans in third with the pair split by the Ferrari of Hawthorn. Moss, victim to another bout of bad luck, had missed a gear change on the first lap of the race and blown his engine in spectacular fashion.

Three weeks later and the teams were back in action once more – this time at the French Grand Prix. With Hawthorn in pole position ahead of Moss and the Ferraris of Wolfgang von Trips and Peter Collins in third and fifth split by the Maserati of Juan-Manuel Fangio, who was racing in his last ever Grand Prix, it was apparent that the Prancing Horse was back on form. Replicating the superb drive of his rival in Holland, Hawthorn held his lead from the start and was never once challenged on his way to taking victory almost 25 seconds ahead of second-placed Moss.

Stirling Moss, left and Mike Hawthorn at Silverstone for the British Grand Prix, July 1958

*Stirling Moss and Mike Hawthorn discussing the Thursday
trials at the British Grand Prix, Silverstone*

Ferrari was able to maintain this new found momentum as the racing moved to Britain and the Silverstone circuit. On this occasion, it was Collins who took victory ahead of his team mate Hawthorn and the Cooper of Salvadori. Moss, meanwhile, was once again a victim of the Vanwall's fragile engine having covered only one third of the distance before going out with mechanical problems. Neither Hawthorn nor Moss could score points on the Nürburgring a fortnight later as both were, again, victims to mechanical failure. However, both were considerably more fortunate than Hawthorn's team mate Collins who was tragically killed when his Ferrari somersaulted after running wide and hitting a ditch.

The following round at an atypically wet Oporto street circuit in Portugal was to become the defining moment of the season. Having qualified in pole position, Moss was quick to take command of the racing order but, as the cars struggled for grip on tramlines and cobbles, it was Hawthorn who soon moved into the lead on lap 2. Regaining control, Moss retook the lead six laps later and continued to dominate for the remainder of the race to take victory ahead of his countryman and rival. But it was soon reported that Hawthorn had infringed the rules by pushing his Ferrari the wrong way after a spin and was, therefore, disqualified. First to protest was Moss. In his characteristically polite but firm manner, he pointed out that, when Hawthorn had pushed his car, it was actually on the pavement and, therefore, no offence had taken place. After considering the plea of the winning driver it was decided to reinstate Hawthorn allowing the original result to stand.

This was to have a dramatic effect as the championship moved into its final round at the Ain-Diab circuit in Morocco. With Hawthorn having placed second during the penultimate round at Monza with Moss once again failing to finish, the championship was down to the wire. Moss knew that he not only had to win but also set the fastest lap of the race to gain an extra point and even this would only secure the championship if Hawthorn finished in third place or below. Moss drove the race of his life – first securing pole then setting the fastest lap and ultimately taking an emphatic victory by almost 85 seconds – but it was Hawthorn who had taken second place and subsequently the title by a single point.

Hawthorn was celebrated as the first English world champion but it would have been a different story had the gentlemanly and sporting conduct of Stirling Moss not handed him the six points that had secured him overall victory. Sadly, Hawthorn's victory was to be short lived when, just three months later, he was killed having lost control of his Jaguar road car on the Guildford bypass in Surrey.

England team captain Bobby Moore holds the cup aloft supported by Nobby Stiles, Jackie Charlton, Alan Ball, Geoff Hurst, Martin Peters, Bobby Charlton, George Cohen, Ray Wilson and Roger Hunt, at the 1966 World Cup, Wembley

1966 WORLD CUP: ENGLAND V WEST GERMANY

With the World Cup finals due to return to Europe and the English Football Association celebrating their centenary in 1963 – easily the longest established football association in the world – there was only one possible venue for the 1966 tournament and England was duly ratified as the host in 1960. This was a time when the England manager was manager in name only, with the squad being selected by a committee and the manager, Walter Winterbottom, expected to make the best out of the players put at his disposal. By the time preparations began for the 1966 World Cup, all that had changed.

The crunch had come after the 1962 tournament, when England had faltered at the quarter-final stage once again. Walter Winterbottom duly resigned after seventeen years in charge of the team and the search began for his replacement. Eventually, the Football Association turned to a former player, Alf Ramsey, then manager at Ipswich Town. But Ramsey would only take the job under his own terms – he and he alone would pick the squad and thereafter the team. While Walter Winterbottom had relied on his previous training as a former wing commander in the RAF to keep the players under control, Alf came across, at least to the players, as one of the lads. "Call me Alf," he answered when asked what they should call him at one of his earliest team get-togethers.

His reign as manager got off to the worst possible start with a 5-2 defeat by France in the 1964 European Championship qualifying tournament, which duly saw England eliminated from the competition. His promise that England would win the World Cup seemed the height of folly, but Alf Ramsey had good reason to believe his side would fare well, not least because for the first time they were spared the inconvenience of having to qualify, joining holders Brazil as the two nations to have automatic qualification for the finals.

Unlike other host countries England decided to use existing grounds on which to play the competition, giving huge grants to those clubs fortunate enough to have their ground selected. The only certainty was that England, regardless of what group they were placed in, would play their matches at Wembley. Group 2 would be played at Villa Park (home of Aston Villa) and Hillsborough (Sheffield Wednesday), the traditional FA Cup semi-final venues. Group 3 would be played at Goodison Park (Everton) and Old Trafford (Manchester United), whilst Group 4 was located at Ayresome Park (Middlesbrough) and Roker Park (Sunderland).

It had been planned that all six matches in Group 1, England's group, would be played at Wembley but, as the tournament grew closer, it suddenly dawned that the stadium was not technically available on the 15th July, when Uruguay were due to meet France, as Wembley would be staging its regular greyhound racing evening. Although the rest of the country had caught World Cup fever, the Greyhound Racing Association refused to cancel their meeting, meaning the FA had to find an alternative venue for the match. Despite the claims of Highbury and White Hart Lane, two London based grounds that could accommodate over 50,000 fans, the FA chose the White City, a venue originally built for the 1908 Olympic Games.

With the trophy in place, assorted dignitaries assembled and the world watching, England kicked off the 1966 World Cup finals against Uruguay on 11th July. Group 1 was won by England, whose 2-0 victories over both Mexico and France ensured them qualification for the next stage, although it was not all plain sailing. The match against France proved especially troublesome, with Nobby Stiles's horrendous challenge on Jacques Simon leading to calls for the player to be expelled from the tournament. It was Alf Ramsey who leapt to the player's defence, stating "if Stiles goes, I go", which had the FA backing down. Jimmy Greaves, perhaps the finest goalscorer of the age, suffered a gash on his shin during the same match, a gash that would keep him out of the next two matches, with disastrous consequences for the player later. Another player who bowed out of the 1966 tournament was Mexican goalkeeper Antonio Carbajal, whose eleven appearances for his country in the finals had come in the 1950, 1954, 1958, 1962 and 1966 competitions, a longevity record unlikely to be challenged in the future, even allowing for the fact that goalkeepers tend to play on for longer than their outfield counterparts.

And so to Wembley for the final. A crowd of 100,000 was crammed into the stadium and some 600 million were watching on television – what they saw and what they have debated ever since has entered folklore. Although Jimmy Greaves had recovered from injury, Alf Ramsey resisted the temptation to bring him back into the side. Whilst popular belief is that Geoff Hurst kept him out of the side, the reality is that Roger Hunt was most at risk at losing his place. Ramsey also decided against recalling any of his wingers, settling on a 4-4-2 formation that made England extremely difficult to score against.

After extra time, German fans in full voice watched closely by an English Policeman

Ramsey's biggest tactical victory however, came from the German decision to assign Franz Beckenbauer to mark Bobby Charlton – Beckenbauer was certainly more than capable of doing the job but it robbed the Germans of his own attacking prowess, which had already netted him four goals.

Both sides started cautiously, perhaps afraid to make a mistake, but after 12 minutes, Ray Wilson made his only one of the tournament, weakly heading out a cross to the unmarked Helmut Haller who shot home the opening goal. Five minutes later, England drew level, Bobby Moore quickly whipping in a free kick for Geoff Hurst to head home whilst the Germans were still organizing their defence. England were the stronger side thereafter and deservedly took the lead with some 12 minutes left on the clock, Alan Ball sending in a corner that ran on to Hurst. His shot was blocked, but it arched up invitingly for Martin Peters to hammer home what appeared to be the decisive winning goal.

With the clock running down, the Germans' efforts became more and more desperate. As the game moved into injury time, Jackie Charlton was harshly penalised for a foul on Held, although Charlton protested his innocence. Emmerich's free kick appeared to be helped on by Schnellinger's hand before arriving at the foot of Weber at the far post and helped over the line for an improbable equalizer. England appeared crestfallen at being robbed so close to the prize, but Ramsey's motivational skills came to the fore. 'You've beaten them once, now go and do it again' he told them. Nearly forty years later, what happened during the first half of extra time is known the length and breadth of the country and debated still. Geoff Hurst received the ball inside the German penalty area, spun and fired a shot goalwards that cannoned off the underneath of the crossbar, bounced down onto the goal line to be greeted with cheers and cries of 'goal' from the England players and crowd. The referee Gottfried Dienst wasn't so sure but decided to consult with the nearest linesman, the Russian Tofik Bakhramov (who according to legend had fought against the Germans during the Second World War!), who had been badly positioned some 10 yards from the goal line and 50 yards from the goal but was convinced enough to signal that he thought it a goal. Had that been the last of the scoring, then the controversy would still be raging today (and in some parts of Germany it no doubt still does!), but in the final moments, Geoff Hurst latched on to a considered clearance from Bobby Moore, ignored the presence of the chasing German defender and a few of the crowd who had run on to the pitch and fired home the fourth and final goal (he also completed the perfect hat trick, scoring with each foot and a header). It is debatable who benefited more from the goal; Geoff Hurst, who scored it, or commentator Kenneth Wolstenholme, whose words 'There are some people on the pitch, they think it's all over – it is now', as Hurst scored, are as much a part of the 1966 folklore as Pickles, Eusebio and Rattin.

Geoff Hurst scores his third goal against West Germany during the 1966 World Cup final match

Captain Bobby Moore made his way up the steps at Wembley for the third consecutive year (he had picked up the FA Cup and European Cup Winners Cup for West Ham in 1964 and 1965) to collect the greatest prize of all, pausing to thoughtfully wipe the sweat off his hand before extending it towards Queen Elizabeth II and receiving the trophy. It was recently claimed, many years after the event, that as Bobby Moore made his way back down to the pitch, the trophy was switched with the replica commissioned by the FA, just in case a thief more audacious than the one who had swooped at Central Hall might be prowling, but with more than a 100,000 witnesses nothing untoward was likely.

Regardless of the claims of the South Americans, who believed England won as a result of a conspiracy, and the debate about the third goal in the final, England were worthy winners, growing in confidence as the competition progressed and reserving their better performances for when it really mattered. More than anything it proved the abilities of manager Alf Ramsey, who took a side that had probably only three, possibly four truly world class players and fashioned all of them into world champions. Just as he said he would when he took over as manager two years previously.

A tense moment during the match

29

1966 JACK NICKLAUS DEFENDS MASTERS AND WINS GRAND SLAM

It had taken the legendary Jack Nicklaus just four years to claim his grand slam victory when he defended his Masters championship title and then won the Open at Muirfield in a dazzling display of talent in 1966. At the time, the Open was the only major tournament to have eluded the golfing giant, but the "Golden Bear", as he was nicknamed, staved off the challenge from Doug Sanders and Dave Thomas to claim the championship in a convincing win. Nicklaus was so pleased with the achievement that he went on to name his own course Muirfield Village in Dublin, Ohio.

It was to be the first of three victories for Nicklaus at the Open. When Thomas and Sanders both took a par at the 17th hole, Nicklaus needed two fours to win. Having been runner-up at the tournament a total of seven times, Nicklaus was determined and on form to win. At the 17th, knowing that not much lay between him and the championship, Nicklaus scored a birdie four and par four on the final two holes to finish one stroke ahead of his rivals.

Nicklaus, born on 21st January 1940, began his road to the Grand Slam when he won the US Open in 1962 beating Arnold Palmer in a play-off. The following year saw him win the Masters with a one-stroke lead over Tony Lema while later, in 1963, he claimed his first PGA Championship title when he triumphed over Dave Ragan Jr with a two-stroke lead. All he needed was the British Open. But 1965 did not prove to be his defining year, although he did win the Masters for the second time with a nine-stroke lead over challengers Arnold Palmer and Gary Player. The Masters was once again

a victory for Nicklaus in 1966 after he found himself up against Gay Brewer and Tommy Jacobs in a play-off that was to see the "Golden Bear" win. However later that same year he proved just how much of a sporting hero he was when he claimed his grand slam.

Hailing from Columbus, Ohio, Nicklaus took up golf at the age of 10 and, by the age of 13, was competent enough on the course to score 70. Three years later saw him claim his first Ohio State Open against professionals in 1956 and within another five years – while still at Ohio State University – he won victories in two US Amateur Championships (1959 and 1961). The 1960 US Open saw Nicklaus as runner-up to Arnold Palmer – only two shots behind and 1959 and 1961 were also the years that he represented the US in the Walker Cup team where he won all his matches. At the time, Nicklaus won the US Open in 1962 – his first year as a professional – beating Arnold Palmer, he was the youngest winner in the history of the tournament. The year was to prove a flying start for the exceptional golfer who went on to win the Seattle Open and the Portland Open that same year. His efforts earned him the "Rookie of the Year" award. Other major tournaments were victories for Nicklaus the following year and, although he did not win any majors during 1964, he did find himself at the top of the tour money list over Arnold Palmer.

Things really took off for him when he won the Masters in 1965 and then again in 1966. It was the first time that any golfer had managed to successfully defend the title. Nicklaus was on the up and, by the time he won the Grand Slam in 1966, he was only the fourth professional to achieve it after Ben Hogan, Gene Sarazen and Gary Player.

Things quietened down for Nicklaus on the world's golf courses after 1967 and he failed to win another major until the British Open in 1970 on the Old Course at St Andrews where he beat rival Doug Sanders in a play-off. (He became a member of the Royal & Ancient Club 20 years later). The following year was to see him win the 1971 PGA Championship which gave Nicklaus the honour of being the first golfer to win all four major championships twice. During the remainder of the 1970s and the 1980s, Nicklaus continued with an

incredible game of golf that contemporaries marvelled at. He joined the Champions Tour at the age of 50 in 1990 and enjoyed success until 1992 which proved to be a winless year for the "Golden Bear". He was back on form the following year and enjoyed a busy decade on the greens.

He came back to compete in the 2005 Masters and finished his sensational career at the Open on the Old Course at St Andrews that same year although he did take part in the US Open and the PGA Championship in 2000. This great sporting hero is also a talented and devoted architect of golf courses and currently has one of the largest golf design companies in the world.

Jack Nicklaus putts out on the 18th hole as Don January looks on. Nicklaus finished this third round of play in the Masters Golf Tournament in a first place tie with Tommy Jacobs

Overleaf: An argument over rules causes a referee to quit

1966 FORMULA ONE WORLD CHAMPIONSHIP

A significant change in the rules heralded the start of the 1966 Formula One World Championship. Since 1961, the maximum permitted capacity of the cars had been limited to just 1500cc but, in a landmark decision, the regulations had been amended to allow the use of engines up to 3.0 litres. Horsepower was back but, just as the move to the smaller capacity had caused chaos and consternation at the start of the 1961 season, so the new changes had thrown many of the manufacturers into turmoil as the first race approached.

Unwilling to develop a 3.0 litre engine, Coventry Climax had announced their withdrawal from competition whilst Lotus, their new Ford Cosworth engine still under development, were forced to use an older design from British manufacturer BRM. Ferrari, meanwhile, had elected to use a shimmed down version of their successful 3.3 litre V12 sportscar engine. Jack Brabham, world champion in 1959 and 1960 and owner of his own team, the Brabham Racing Organisation, chose to commission Repco, the Australian engineering firm with whom he shared their Surbiton premises, to produce an engine of his own based upon an obsolete V8 Oldsmobile production engine. This decision would prove to pay dividends as the season progressed.

The opening race at Monaco was a shambolic affair. Such was the lack of preparedness that even reigning champion Jim Clark was forced to drive a year-old car fitted with a 2-litre Climax engine, although this failed to prevent the superlative Scot from taking pole position from the Ferrari 312 of John Surtees with the BRMs of Hill and Stewart relegated to third and fourth. However, as the race started it was Surtees who surged ahead into the first corner making good use of his additional horsepower. Surtees continued to lead the procession until lap 16 when his transmission failed forcing him to retire. He was soon followed first by Brabham with gearbox problems and then by Spence, Rindt and Clark as one by one the hard twisting nature of the course got the better of the poorly tested machinery. By the time Jackie Stewart's BRM victoriously crossed the finish line ahead of Bandini's Ferrari, only six cars were still running, and two of these, the Cooper-Maseratis of Ligier and Bonnier, were so far distant and 25 laps down that they failed to be classified.

Not a single car suffered a mechanical failure at the next round of the championship held on a rain soaked Spa circuit in Belgium but unfortunately this phenomenon was not down to some miracle advance in automotive engineering. As torrential conditions swept across the track no less than eight of the 15 starters were involved in two separate crashes on the opening lap. With rain limiting visibility to nothing more than a few feet, first Bonnier, Spence, Siffert and Hulme collided at Burnenville and then Stewart, Hill, Bondurant and Clarke were forced off at the Masta Kink. Stewart suffered a broken shoulder after being trapped upside down in his BRM but his injuries could have been far worse had Hill not valiantly pulled the petrol drenched driver from his upturned car. Ultimately it was Surtees who overcame the horrendous conditions to take victory from Rindt, Bandini and Brabham.

Surtees's victory at Spa was to be his last for Ferrari. Angered by internal politics, he walked out on the team at the Le Mans 24 hour. As the Formula 1 championship moved on to Reims for the French Grand Prix, he was back in action – this time behind the wheel of a Cooper-Maserati. His efforts were, however, somewhat short-lived when, after having qualified second, he sped away from the start to take the lead on the first lap and then suffered a fuel pump failure forcing him to abandon. After a hard fought race, Jack Brabham took victory from Surtees' Ferrari replacement Briton Mike Parkes. Brabham's unique Repco engine had come good at last. The Australian's winning ways continued at the British Grand Prix held at Brands Hatch where he led a Brabham-Repco one-two with team mate Denny Hulme although it

should be mentioned that their closest rivals, Ferrari, were unable to attend due to the strikes that were blighting Italian industry. The Maranello racers were, however, back in action as the championship moved on to the Dutch circuit of Zandvoort but once again it was the Brabham pairing who set the pace by taking the first two places on the grid. With the press speculating that Brabham was too old to win the championship for a third time many were amused at the sight of the 40-year-old Australian limping to his car with the aid of a walking stick and a stick-on false beard! For all his joking, Brabham was more than aware that the only true way to silence the doubters was to prove them wrong and this he did by winning the Grand Prix from Graham Hill, who was over a lap behind, and Jim Clark who was distanced by two laps. It was one of the most absolute victories in Grand Prix history.

German GP at Nürburgring, 1966

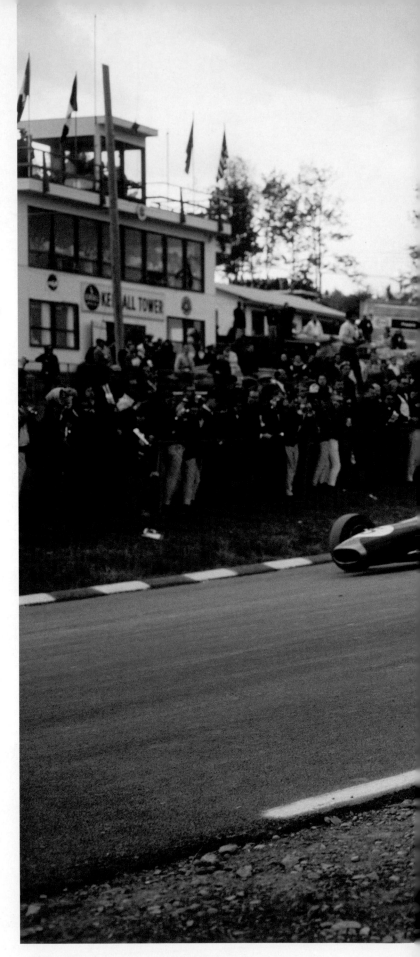

Brabham continued his winning streak two weeks later at the notorious Nürburgring. Moving to the front on the first lap after qualifying in fifth place his lead was never challenged as the cars swept along the narrow strip of tarmac across the Eifel Mountains.

When the championship moved to Monza a month later it was already clear that the only person in a position to challenge Brabham for the title was Cooper-Maserati's John Surtees. As the drivers battled hard in the opening laps, it appeared to be business as usual when the Australian moved to the front on lap four but when mechanical difficulties forced him to retire at the end of the seventh lap the fight for the title was blown wide open. Brabham sat nervously in the pits watching his rival as the race progressed. Surtees had moved up to fourth place behind Scarfiotti, Parkes and Hulme when he entered the pit lane for an unscheduled stop. Climbing out of his cockpit it was clear that Surtees' race was run – his car having developed a fuel leak.

With two races still left to run, Brabham was declared 1966 champion and in doing so became the first and only driver in Grand Prix history to win the title in a car bearing his own name – a record that in this day and age is never likely to be equalled.

The grid rolls off on a parade lap before the start of the 1966 US Grand Prix at Watkins Glen, NY. Jack Brabham (#5) on left in his Brabham-Repco, Lorenzo Bandini (#9) in his red Ferrari 312 and John Surtees (#7) is on the right in his Cooper-Maserati

1967 ITALIAN GRAND PRIX: MONZA

Before a wheel had turned, it was obvious that the 1967 Italian Grand Prix was destined to be one of the classic races of all time. At the sharp end of the action, New Zealand-born Chris Amon was ready to showcase the 48-valve V12 powered Ferrari 312 whilst Honda, having missed the Canadian round some two weeks earlier, was set to field British ace John Surtees in its new RA300 - a thundering machine, affectionately known as the Hondola, which utilized the company's brutal new V12 motor on a lightweight Lola chassis that had been built for the Indianapolis 500. Meanwhile Dan Gurney's AAR Eagle-Weslake was equipped with a new, stronger engine which also showed promise. However, it was Jim Clark's unstoppable Cosworth-DFV engined Lotus 49 that proved to be the one to beat come qualification.

Setting out early in the opening session the Scottish farmer from Fife posted a phenomenal 1:28.5 seconds for his 3.57 mile lap of the Monza circuit - a stunning average speed of 145.2mph - whilst 0.3 seconds in arrears was Jack Brabham driving his eponymous BT24-Repco. Third on the grid was Bruce McLaren's BRM powered M5A closely followed by the Ferrari of Amon and Gurney's Eagle. Five different cars were to take the first five places on the starting grid for this Italian epic.

As was typical for any race at the Autodromo Nazionale the start was utter chaos. The flag had not even had the chance to drop before Clark's fellow front-row men sped away with smoke pouring from their tyres. The field soon gave chase but by the end of the first lap it was Australian Brabham who held the lead closely pursued by Gurney and the Lotus of Graham Hill. Clarke, meanwhile, was in fourth having pushed his way back past McLaren's M5A, Jackie Stewart's BRM and Denny Hulme's Brabham-Repco following the opening mêlée. It was then Gurney's turn to briefly take control before Clark finally moved into the lead on the third lap. Gurney tried to stay in contact but was forced to retire on lap five when his Weslake V12 motor expired.

Jack Brabham in his Brabham Repco in the grid at Monza before the 1967 Italian Grand Prix

Jack Brabham at the Italian Grand Prix, Monza, 1967

It was now the twin Lotuses of Clark and Hill that led the pair of Brabhams followed closely by Stewart who could see a battle royal unfolding behind him as McLaren, Amon, Surtees and Scarfiotti fought for position on every corner. Next to take the initiative was Hulme who put in a lap record of 1:28.9 to push his Brabham into the lead just as, further down the field, the great Jochen Rindt took advantage of the confusion to move his Cooper-Maserati into fifth. Hulme's hold of the lead was brief as, once more, Clark applied the pressure and retook the initiative. Clark wanted this win and wanted it badly. But then disaster struck when, without any warning, the Lotus's handling became erratic and the back started drifting out on each corner. Clark had punctured while leading.

Hulme took the lead once more as the Scotsman dived into the pits for an unscheduled wheel change.

But, whereas a modern F1 car's wheel can be changed in about half the time it takes you to read this sentence, in 1967, it was a more laboured affair. By the time he was able to rejoin the action Clark was a whole lap down behind his third placed Lotus team mate. Hill and Clark soon took advantage of their more powerful machinery to pass Brabham and it was left to the Englishman to jockey for position with Hulme. The lead changed between the two drivers six times within the next 15 laps but it was too much for Denny Hulme's Brabham and he was forced to retire on lap 30 having overheated.

Once again the Lotus duo took the initiative as Clark moved past Hill and put in lap after blistering lap – breaking the track record with a time equal to that which had earned him his pole position. Dragging along Hill in his slipstream, Brabham was left trailing

Brabham Strealine in Italian GP practice

by a country mile. With 58 of the 68 laps behind them, Clark was set to overtake third placed John Surtees in the Honda when disaster struck once more but this time it was Hill's turn for misfortune as his engine expired in spectacular fashion. Unfazed, Clark completed his manoeuvre and all of a sudden found himself in second place behind Jack Brabham. With the bit firmly between his teeth, he continued to push hard and, to the amazement of all watching, he passed the Australian to take the lead on his 61st circuit having un-lapped himself.

Fate, however, was about to play a cruel hand. With just two corners remaining on the final lap the Lotus started to cough and splutter as the pumps desperately gasped for fuel that wasn't there and Clark could do nothing as he watched Surtees' Honda and Brabham's Repco come storming past in the closing yards to take the top two steps on the podium with just 0.2 seconds separating them. Clark's Lotus rolled in under its own momentum 23 seconds later.

Although Clark's drive may ultimately have been for little reward, there is no doubt that it was, and remains to be, one of the greatest achievements in the history of Grand Prix racing.

Jacky Ickx, Cooper-Maserati, drives through the Parabolica, Italian Grand Prix, Monza, 1967

Jim Clark besides his Lotus-Cosworth 49 on the grid before the Italian Grand Prix, Monza 1967

Jackie Stewart and Chris Amon, 1967

Tony Jacklin and his wife Vivien kiss the claret jug Golf Champion trophy, while he holds the gold medal after winning the 1969 Open Championship

1969
BRITISH OPEN: TONY JACKLIN

Quite simply, Tony Jacklin was the hero of British golf from 1969 to 1972. He popularized the sport for the masses in the UK with his epic win at the Open in 1969 then again when he went on to triumph at the US Open in 1970. This made him the first player to hold both British and US titles simultaneously since 1953 when Ben Hogan was champion of both.

No British player had won the Open since Max Faulkner in 1951 – but Jacklin was about to change all that. Born in Scunthorpe on 7th July 1944, Jacklin was a keen golfer from an early age. His style developed well and he was decisive and expertly controlled his game from 100 yards inwards. He possessed an aggressive style of attack which made him formidable against opponents but his parents were worried about him becoming a professional, with the risks it involved, despite his resounding successes at the Lincolnshire Championships.

At Royal Lytham, spectators were anxious for an exciting result. Jacklin scored impressively in the first and second rounds with 68 and 70 respectively and, by the third, round he was only three strokes behind Bob Charles – the Open Champion of 1963. By the final round, Jacklin had increased his form enough to be two strokes ahead of Charles. Bob Charles watched as his ball went into the rough on the final hole, while Jacklin sent his drive down the middle of the fairway. Charles was back on the green by his second shot but Jacklin's second shot took him closer to the green.

It took Jacklin just two putts to triumph over rival Charles and take the 1969 Championship. As a result of his achievement – he was the first British golfer to win the tournament in 18 years – Jacklin's popularity soared and the British public took up golf, watched golf, practised golf and breathed golf in their droves.

He was the Arnold Palmer – one of his own heroes – of the British game. Jacklin was in with a chance of winning the Open once again in 1972 when he and Lee Trevino tied for the lead one stroke ahead of Jack Nicklaus at the 17th hole. Jacklin was in just as much disbelief as everyone else – including Trevino – when Trevino's ball (which had hit the upslope behind the green) was hit by a frustrated challenger who watched as the ball rolled straight into the hole for a par.

Not only did Jacklin hit the heights with his brilliant win at the Open in 1969, but he also impressed the world of golf with his outstanding performance in the Ryder Cup of that same year. This was also one of the most memorable performances in the Ryder Cup's history and is known to golf fans the world over as "The Concession". It was down to Jacklin and his fellow competitor in the final singles match of the tournament to decide which side of the Atlantic would be celebrating a win. Not fazed by the magnitude of the moment, Jacklin kept his cool to deliver a 50-foot eagle putt at the 17th at Royal Birkdale which put the British and Irish team in good contention for the title. It led to a tie – the first for the Ryder Cup – although Nicklaus retained the Cup for the US. It was a moving and memorable moment when two golfing giants walked off the 18th green with their arms around each other's

Jacklin putting on the 18th green to win the British Open

shoulders. This is probably one of the greatest shows of professionalism ever and is widely regarded by all who witnessed it as a grand gesture of true sportsmanship.

Jacklin became the Ryder Cup captain for the British and Irish team in 1983. This role was to transform the tournament into what it has become today and no other player in the history of the Cup has done more than Jacklin to see it transcend to the heady heights it occupies in the golfing calendar. Indeed, for Jacklin, "The Ryder Cup is more than just golf. It is your country, your team, your tour, your captain, you're playing for it...it is the ultimate in golf". When Jacklin took over the captaincy in 1983, the US team had been, and still was, threatening to dominate the tournament. Although the British and Irish lost that year it somehow ignited a fire – fanned by Jacklin – for the team to succeed in the future. Two years later Jacklin was an inspiration for his team as non-playing captain and the British team won the Ryder Cup for the first time in 28 years.

Jacklin holds up the claret jug Golf Champion trophy and the gold medal

1970 WORLD CUP: MEXICO

The contest to host the 1970 World Cup finals was a two-horse race between Mexico and Argentina, with the latter pointing out their slightly better pedigree in the competition. They also pointed out that they had put forward a compelling case for hosting the 1962 tournament, only to be beaten by Chile in the final reckoning. There was to be further disappointment for Argentina this time too, for at the 1964 Olympic Games in Tokyo, FIFA ratified the choice of Mexico as hosts for the World Cup, a decision taken because Mexico was already hosting the 1968 Olympic Games.

The decision, extremely unpopular within Argentina, was not greeted with much enthusiasm elsewhere either, not least because it meant that competing teams would have to contend with blistering heat and high altitude. Add to this the, at times, volatile tournaments that had taken place in 1962 and 1966, especially when a South American side had faced a European one and there were those contemplating little more than a perpetual bloodbath. They needn't have worried, for the 1970 World Cup finals turned out to be one of the most exciting, adventurous and enjoyable competitions both before and since.

Both England and Mexico were spared the difficulty of having to qualify, being given safe passage as holders and hosts respectively (although just as in 1966, both were in the hat for the qualification process, England being assigned Group 9 and Mexico Group 14, the only teams in their groups). For once the number of entrants fell, down by one from the previous tournament at seventy nations. Europe's thirty applicants were given a total of nine places (eight plus England), South America's ten countries received three places, the Central and North American Federation CONCACAF's twelve entries given two places (one plus Mexico), Asia/Oceania's seven nations afforded one place, as were the eleven African countries.

Many countries made it known that they would not play against Israel. As a result, the team was placed in the Asia/Oceania sub-group B with North Korea and New Zealand, but North Korea were eliminated from the group for refusing to play Israel. The Israelis beat New Zealand home and away to qualify for the final, a meeting with Australia. Australia's route to the final had also been rocked with political issues; their second round match against Rhodesia had to be played in Mozambique because no country recognised Rhodesia and would not travel to the country for fixtures! Australia finally won after a play-off but lost out to Israel in the final, losing 1-0 away and only drawing 1-1 at home. Israel, the country no one wanted to play, qualified for the finals in Mexico.

The real drama came in the CONCACAF section, where the thirteen original entrants were placed into four groups, the four winners moving into a knockout stage. Haiti beat the USA home and away to book their place in the final, whilst the other tie between Honduras and El Salvador needed a third match before El Salvador finally won 3-2, but so intense had been the clash the two countries went to war for four days in the immediate aftermath! Although the skirmish became known as the Football War, there had been

Gerd Muller and Uwe Seeler at the World Cup Football finals 1970 in Leon

border disputes between the two countries previously; football provided a convenient excuse for some pent-up frustration being released.

Brazil won their group in South America with a 100% record, offering proof that they would be a force to be reckoned with come the finals. They were joined by Peru who, inspired by Brazilian manager Didi, saw off the Argentineans and Uruguay.

According to England manager Sir Alf Ramsey (he was knighted after England's triumph in 1966), he had an even better squad in 1970 than that that had won

the competition four years earlier. Only six of the 1966 winners were still regulars in the side, but the likes of Gordon Banks and Bobby Moore had actually improved their reputations and stature in the game following that victory. England's preparations for the tournament commenced more than a year before the tournament kicked off with something of a fact-finding mission into South America with matches against Mexico, Uruguay and Brazil. While the results were at best mediocre (England drew 0-0 with Mexico, beat Uruguay 2-1 and lost to Brazil by the same score), it was Ramsey's attitude that would cause problems.

His abrasive style was not appreciated by either the local populace or journalists in Mexico and would be paid back with interest when the competition proper kicked off.

The competition kicked off with a spectacular opening ceremony involving some 50,000 balloons and a drab match between Mexico and the USSR that was high on yellow cards but low on action – it finished goalless. The only way after that was up, and all sixteen teams played their part in turning the competition into a true feast of football.

After their stale opening, both the Mexicans and Russians improved, finishing joint group winners ahead of Belgium and El Salvador. The Russians were given top place thanks to having scored one more goal than the Mexicans, but the hosts did not concede a goal in any of their three matches.

England also found goals difficult to come by, opening their campaign with a 1-0 win over Romania courtesy of a Geoff Hurst goal. The Brazilians showed how they were going to dominate the group with a 4-1 demolition of Czechoslovakia, with Pelé, much better protected than he had been in 1966, new revelation Jairzinho and centre forward Tostao, who had recovered from a potentially career-threatening eye injury, particularly impressive. Indeed, the highlight of the match was a shot that didn't go in – Pelé spotting the goalkeeper off his line and firing goalwards from the halfway line!

The two giants of Group 3 met five days later in one of the most eagerly anticipated of all World Cup matches. England's task wasn't helped by the fact that a Mexican crowd had camped outside their headquarters the night before and chanted and honked their car horns in order to disrupt the players' sleep – midway through the night the squad had to be moved to another part of the hotel. With television such a dominant part of the

proceedings the kick off was scheduled for midday, a time when the heat and the sun would be at their highest. Although England in particular were not used to such conditions the two sides produced something of a classic, with the battle between Pelé and Bobby Moore perhaps one of the finest man to man clashes ever produced in world football. Moore had his best game in an England shirt, Pelé produced a few flashes of brilliance but they were both eventually eclipsed by Gordon Banks, who produced a breathtaking save from a Pelé header that even had Pelé applauding. Brazil did find a way through thanks to Jairzinho, but England also had chances; Astle missed a virtual open goal and Alan Ball hit the bar. When the final whistle sounded and Pelé and Moore swapped shirts, most of the watching world was convinced the two sides would be meeting again in the final. Both made sure of their progress into the quarter-finals, England beating Czechoslovakia 1-0 through a penalty from Allan Clarke and Brazil beat Romania 3-2.
The quarter-finals saw the Uruguayans finally get the better of the Russians with a goal in extra time, but it was the three other ties that provided the drama. In Toluca home interest in the competition was ended with a 4-1 victory for Italy, finally finding their goalscoring form. The match was not as one-sided as the scoreline suggests, for the two sides were level at half time and only the Italians' experience pulled them through in the second half.

Despite frantic charges from England in their match against West Germany, no goals were forthcoming in the final minutes, and England slipped out of the competition, not to return for a further twelve years. Rather than freshen Bobby Charlton for future matches, the substitution brought down the curtain on an international career that had stretched for 106 matches and brought 49 goals, a record.

On paper, the meeting between Brazil and Italy in the World Cup final was as much a meeting of styles, with the defensive capabilities of the Italians, the semi-final notwithstanding, being the main reason for their progress to the final. By contrast, the Brazilians had a defence that was at best suspect, being protected largely by the delights that were the midfield and attack. It was not Brito, or Piazza or even Felix that would win the trophy for Brazil, rather what the likes of Pelé, Jairzinho and Tostao could do at the other end. In the 17th minute Rivelino sent in an inviting cross and Pelé rose to head home powerfully at the foot of the post for the game's opening goal. Italy got back into the game eight minutes before the interval after the Brazilians were guilty of sloppiness, gifting the ball to Boninsegna to round Felix and strike home an equalizer.

Capable of better, the Brazilians finally proved it in the second half. Gerson beat one defender and fired home a powerful shot from outside the penalty area with his left foot. Gerson was involved in the third goal, firing in a long ball that was headed down by Pelé into the path of Jairzinho that roared into the net, giving Jairzinho the honour of becoming the first and still only player to have scored in every match of the finals. Three minutes from time came the final goal, Pelé this time feeding captain and defender Carlos Alberto to fire home another long range effort. It was the performance that the world had wanted and the result the purists dreamed of, but the Italians put on a display that did themselves justice – against almost anyone else they might have won, but this was the Brazilians in 1970, perhaps the best side the world has ever seen.

In winning the trophy for the third time, Brazil won it for the last time – it had been decided that whoever won the competition three times would get to keep the Jules Rimet Trophy forever. Although Italy could have achieved the feat, it was Carlos Alberto who became the last captain to hold the trophy aloft, at the same time that manager Mario Zagalo became the first man to win the World Cup as a player and manager. It was the end of the Jules Rimet Trophy (subsequently stolen in Brazil and believed to have been melted down for its gold content), the end of Pelé in the competition and the end of an era. It could not have had a more fitting finale.

Pele goes past a Czechoslovakian defender during the World Cup, Mexico, 1970

1971 BRITISH LIONS WIN IN NEW ZEALAND

While the British Lions had registered two previous victories over the New Zealand All Blacks – 6-3 in June 1930 and 9-6 in September 1959 – the 34-man squad that ventured to the southern hemisphere in 1971 was to surpass all expectations.

Although combined British and Irish teams had participated in unofficial tours of Australia and New Zealand since 1888, it was not until 1930 that the Lions officially engaged the All Blacks on their home turf. The first Lions tour with players selected from all four Home Nations took place in South Africa in 1910 but it was not until the inter-war years that the team became known as the Lions, so named after the crest on their jerseys.

Coach Carwyn James built the core of the team around the backbone of the Wales side that had won that year's Five Nations Grand Slam with John Dawes, JPR Williams, Gerald Davies, Mike Gibson, Gareth Edwards and Barry John appearing in all four Tests. In total, 14 Welshmen were selected for the squad, with eight from England and six each from Scotland and Ireland.

In the early stages of the first Test in Dunedin, scrum-half Gareth Edwards limped off to be replaced by fellow Welshman Ray "Chico" Hopkins who went on to play out of his skin. The first points of the game came when the Lions won a line-out and the ball eventually found its way into the hands of John Bevan, who crashed through the New Zealand defence before spilling the ball. When Alan Sutherland attempted to clear his line, Scottish loosehead prop Ian "Mighty Mouse" McLaughlan was there to charge the ball down and claim a try for the visitors. Although fly-half Barry John failed with the conversion, it was his kicking that kept the tourists in the game. As well as helping relieve the pressure on his defence with quality balls down the line, he successfully kicked two penalties to give the Lions a 9-3 victory after full-back Fergie McCormick had equalized for New Zealand with another penalty kick.

The second Test, a fortnight later, saw the All Blacks gain revenge for the opening defeat with a 22-12 triumph although the Lions scored a classic try when full-back JPR Williams collected a high New Zealand clearance deep in his own half. Immediately launching a counterattack, Williams found Gibson in support who in turn laid the ball off to Gerald Davies. The winger sprinted 25 yards to the line to round off a textbook manoeuvre. Not to be outdone, the All Blacks flanker Ian Kirkpatrick broke from a maul near the half-way line and pounded his way to the line, evading all attempts to stop him.

JPR Williams of the British Lions takes on New Zealand's Ian Kirkpatrick during a test match on the British Lions Tour to New Zealand in 1971

All Blacks half-back Sid Going is about to be 'wrapped up' by Lions winger John Bevan (left) and lock forward Willie John McBride during the British Lions V New Zealand first test match

Winning the toss at the start of the third Test in Wellington, the Lions decided to play with the wind in the first half and that would prove to be an inspired decision. Within minutes, the Lions turned over the All Blacks who had won a line-out near their goal-line and Gerald Davies scored the first try of the game. Minutes later, a line-out in nearly the same position on the right wing was palmed down by John Taylor into the path of Gareth Edwards. He jinked past a couple of New Zealand challenges before handing the ball to Barry John for an easy try by the post. With John converting the two tries and adding a drop goal, the score at the end of the first half stood at 13-0 to the Lions. In the second half, the Lions restricted the All Blacks to one try, scored by full-back Laurie Mains. This victory meant that the Lions could not now lose the series and had everything to play for in the fourth and final Test.

Things started well for the All Blacks in Auckland when Wayne Cottrell powered over the line to score the first try of the game. Main successfully kicked the conversion and added a penalty to give the home side

an 8-0 lead. But the Lions were not out of the contest and flanker Peter Dixon reduced the deficit, scoring a try just before half-time with Barry John restoring parity with the conversion and a penalty by the interval.

Shortly after the game had restarted, John gave the visitors the lead with another penalty before Tom Lister scored the All Blacks' second try to level the scores at 11 apiece. It was full-back JPR Williams who stunned the watching world when he attempted a drop goal from just inside his opponents' half. The 45-yard kick flew straight between the posts and for the last 25 minutes the Lions were forced to defend against the All Black tide. As it turned out, the only score they could add was a Mains penalty to level at 14-14 and the visitors rejoiced at the end of the match, having won the series 2-1.

British Lions scrum half Gareth Edwards starts the movement which ended with loose forward Peter Dixon going over for a try. Wayne Cottrell of the All Blacks slows Edwards, with Alex Wyllie (rear) and Ian Kirkpatrick also racing in on the action. Lions flanker John Taylor backs up

1971 ENGLAND REGAIN ASHES IN AUSTRALIA

In the long history of Anglo-Australian rivalry, two bald measurements reflect the achievement of Ray Illingworth's side in 1970/71. He was the first captain since Douglas Jardine, in 1932/33, to win the Ashes back Down Under, and the feat has not been emulated since. So it is the one occasion in 73 years – and counting – that the deed has been done. It also ended Australia's 12-year custody of the urn, which they had regained under Richie Benaud in 1958/59.

Ahead of the tour, Illingworth considered England's chances to be very good, after they did rather better against a star-studded Rest of the World team in 1970 than the 1-4 scoreline suggested. Bill Lawry's Australia, meanwhile, had been trounced 4-0 in South Africa a year earlier. England's aim was to win through pace. It mattered not that their spearhead finished unimpressively in the 1970 domestic averages; John Snow was born to play Test cricket, and the sight of a baggy green cap at the crease provided him with a more rousing motivation than day-in, day-out county cricket.

If Snow was the key bowler in 1970/71, Geoff Boycott was the most influential batsman. After Snow, who was to take 31 wickets in the series, had begun with a six for 114 in the drawn first Test at Brisbane, Boycott produced solid innings of 70 and 50 in the second at Perth, which also ended without result. The third at Melbourne was completely washed out, leading to the rapid organization of the first one-day international. To Illingworth's irritation, an extra Test was also scheduled in at the MCG for later in the tour.

Meanwhile, at Sydney, England went one up, largely through Boycott (77 and 142) and Snow at his quickest, who tore through the hosts in their second innings with seven for 40.

Draws followed at Melbourne and Adelaide, after which Australia, for the first time in 70 years, dropped their captain. Lawry was replaced for the final Test back at the SCG by Ian Chappell, and England, without Boycott, whose arm had been broken by Graham McKenzie in a one-day match just four days earlier, were put in on a bowler-friendly surface. They made just 184, but picked up two quick wickets late on to set up the most dramatic day of the rubber. With Australia closing in despite the loss of seven wickets, Terry Jenner, more spin bowler than batsman, ducked into a short ball from Snow and was hit on the head.

With the crowd erupting after Jenner had been helped off, bringing back memories of 1932/33, Snow was cautioned by umpire Lou Rowan for short-pitched bowling. After a drinks interval in which cans were thrown on to the outfield, Snow went down to field at long leg, where he was briefly grabbed by a drunken spectator. With bottles now being thrown as well as cans, Illingworth led his team off, refusing to return until the ground was cleared and his team's safety assured. Play eventually resumed after a delay of just seven minutes.

Australia took their innings into day three, building a lead of 80, and England's second-innings total of 302 left the hosts needing 223 to win, their only chance of retaining the Ashes.

Again the drama revolved around Snow who, after yorking Ken Eastwood in his first over, dislocated a finger attempting a catch, a mishap that ended his involvement in the match.

After Peter Lever accounted for Ian Chappell, Illingworth decided to bowl himself, ushering in his finest hour as England's captain. At 71, Ian Redpath was held at short leg, and at 82, Doug Walters rose to the young Bob Willis' bait, slashing a wide one to deep gully, placed for the purpose. After Keith Stackpole fell trying to sweep Illingworth, Australia were 123 for five at stumps.

The key batsman at the start of the final day, with 100 needed, was the captain's hugely talented younger brother. Greg Chappell advanced down the wicket and missed Illingworth's out-floater for Alan Knott – whose brilliance behind the stumps had bolstered England throughout – to complete the stumping. Two wickets for Basil D'Oliveira followed before, shortly after 12.30 on 17th February, Keith Fletcher held Jenner at silly point off Underwood. England had won by 62 runs, taking the series 2-0 to regain the Ashes.

A brace of Johns – Edrich and Hampshire – were the two strong men who hoisted Illingworth onto their shoulders and bore the captain from the arena for the presentation. Boycott and Snow – the former with his left arm in a sling, the latter with his right – were both there to savour the ceremony. Not for the first time or the last, Illingworth had revelled in the pressure of a tight situation, guiding his young team to a triumph unique in their lifetimes.

Bill Lawry the Australian Captain (L) and the England Captain Ray Illingworth (R) toss the coin before the forth test in the Ashes series of 1970-71

A victorious England team carry their captain Ray Illingworth off the field after clinching the Ashes by a 62 run win in the 7th Test Match in Sydney

MUNICH OLYMPICS: MARK SPITZ

For all their athletic success, the Berlin Olympics of 1936 are forever tainted by the dark shadow of Nazi Germany. It is difficult to look at a photograph of those Games without your attention being drawn to a military uniform or a swastika flag. As the opening of the 1972 Munich Games drew near, the German nation - all too aware of these connotations - set to ensuring these games would be the greatest in history.

On 26th August 1972, the Games of the XX Olympiad were declared open as German athlete Gunther Zahn lit the Olympic flame. With 7,173 athletes from 121 nations attending, a record on both counts, it seemed that the German organizers had achieved their goal.

Mark Spitz displays the five gold medals he won in the 1972 Olympics

The games continued in peace and harmony for a further nine days until the early hours of 5th September.

Between the hours of four and five, members of the Palestinian terrorist organization Black September entered an apartment building at 31 Connolly Straße in the Olympic Village. It was here that members of the Israeli team were sleeping. As the terrorists stormed the accommodation, wrestling trainer Moshe Weinberger was gunned down and killed. Weightlifter Yossef Romano was then shot as he tried to raise the alarm. Romano died later that day from his wounds. Only three Israeli athletes managed to escape, the remaining nine athletes and officials were taken hostage.

The terrorists published their demands: the unconditional release of 234 Palestinians detained in Israel and safe passage for themselves out of Germany. Avery Brundage, chairman of the IOC announced that "the Games must go on" but, with the situation worsening, competition was suspended at 3:51pm.

Negotiations took place all through the day then, finally, at 10:10pm, the terrorists and their hostages emerged from the apartments to board a waiting coach which in turn transported them to three nearby helicopters. As the helicopters took off, the German authorities entered the building to find the body of Weinberger and three Palestinian's suffering from serious stab wounds.

The helicopters flew to meet a waiting Boeing 727 at Füerstenfeldbruck military airbase. Once on the ground, as the terrorists ushered their prisoners towards the waiting airliner, concealed German snipers opened fire. The intention was simple: kill the terrorists and free the hostages. Despite early reports to the contrary, things had gone badly wrong. In the gun battle that followed, all nine Israeli athletes, five terrorists and a policeman were killed. Incredibly, considering the location and the security involved, three members of Black September escaped.

The next day a crowd of 80,000 attended a memorial service at the Olympic stadium. Avery Brundage insisted that "peace must prevail over violence" so it was announced that the games would continue one day behind schedule.

In spite of the horrific events of 5th September, there were some true athletic highlights at the Munich Games. Within a single week, 22-year-old American swimmer Mark Spitz won an incredible seven gold medals with a world record time in each event. This success took his career Olympic medal tally to 11 medals, nine of them gold.

A 17-year-old Belarusian, Olga Korbut, won the hearts of all who watched her as she recovered from failure to take two gold medals and one silver in the Gymnastics competition. Another young athlete, West German Ulrike Meyfarth, won the women's high jump competition at the age of 16 becoming the youngest winner of an individual athletics event in Olympic history.

Chaos and controversy reigned supreme as the USA and the USSR met in the basketball final. With three seconds remaining, a trailing USA were awarded two free throws. Both scored and the Americans took the lead 50-49. With a single second remaining Soviet coach Vladimir Kondrashkin ran to the referee insisting that he had called a time-out and had not been heard.

At the insistence of the FIBA chairman, a time-out was given but as the two seconds had not been put back on the clock, the buzzer immediately sounded. The Americans were jubilant, their fans invading the court. However, the FIBA chairman once again intervened insisting the missing three seconds be put back on the clock. The time was reset allowing the Russians to inbound the ball straight to Aleksandr Belov who scored unopposed. For the first time ever, the American basketball team had been defeated.

Seven times swimming gold medallist Mark Spitz (second right) during the Olympic Games in Munich

Tom Bruce (L) and Mike Stamm (R) carry teammate Mark Spitz on their shoulders during the medal ceremony for their victory in the men's 4x100-metre medley relay race

1973 BARBARIANS: TRY OF THE CENTURY

When the Barbarians took on New Zealand at Cardiff Arms Park on 27th January 1973, many hoped for a repeat performance of the British Lions victory two years earlier but few were expecting such a marvellous game. While the All Blacks were still a major force to be reckoned with, they had already lost three games – against Llanelli 3-9, North-Western Counties 14-16 and Midlands Counties (West) 8-16 – on their tour of North America, the British Isles and France.

For many people, mention of this game brings to mind the try that was scored after the first few minutes that has since been labelled the "Try of the Century" or simply "the Try". But that is not the whole story of the game, a game that has been acclaimed as one of the best examples of attacking and counterattacking rugby the world has ever seen. "People tend only to remember the first four minutes of the game because of the try," confesses Gareth Edwards, "but what they forgot is the great deal of good rugby played afterwards, much of which came from the All Blacks."

The Barbarians are an invitational rugby team, where the only qualifications are that the player is of a sufficiently high standard and that he has behaved himself both on and off the pitch. The concept had come from William Percy Carpmael in 1890 and the Baa Baas' first game was a 9-4 victory over Hartlepool Rovers on 27 December. There is traditionally one uncapped player picked in every team and, while the players wear their own club socks, the team play in black and white hoops.

The club's motto – "Rugby Football is a game for gentleman in all classes, but for no bad sportsman in any class" – was given to the club by original member and former Bishop of Bloemfontein WJ Carey and all players concur that becoming a Barbarian is one of the greatest achievements in the game. The club's philosophy is one of an attacking game with plenty of flowing rugby and lots of tries.

In 1948, the Home Unions asked the Barbarians to put together a team to play the touring Australia and the Final Challenge was born, traditionally the last match played by an Australian, New Zealand or South African side visiting this country. And so, on 27th January 1973, the Barbarians faced their Final Challenge. The preparations for the game had not gone well for the Barbarians, with players unusually dropping passes in training, and both Gerald Davies and Mervyn Davies had to withdraw through injury and illness.

Following some early skirmishes the All Blacks cleared the ball and Phil Bennett collected it in front of his own posts. Starting off on a jinking run, he soon unloaded the ball to JPR Williams who managed to release the ball to John Pullin as he was tackled. He passed to John Dawes who set off towards the All Black line before passing to the uncapped Tom David. He threw the ball to Derek Quinnell who looked to be passing to David Buckham but Gareth Edwards collected the ball at speed and sprinted the rest of the way to the try-line to put the Barbarians 4-0 up.

Although Phil Bennett failed with the conversion, the Baa Baas continued to rack up the points in the first half. On the half-hour mark, Bennett scored a penalty from 25 yards before they scored their second try of the game when Furgus Slattery collected a loose ball from New Zealand's scrum 10 yards out and touched down to make it 11-0. Bennett again converted and, two minutes later, it was John Bevan who fended off several All Black challenges to score the Barbarians third try and send them into the half-time interval with a 17-0 lead.

The All Blacks hit back following the break with a 25-yard penalty from full-back Joe Karam after Edwards had been penalised for not feeding the ball straight into the scrum. Two minutes later, winger Grant Batty was on the end of an All Black move that had come from winning a Barbarians line-out to score a try that reduced the deficit to 10 points. It was Batty who scored New Zealand's second try with 10 minutes to go, brilliantly rounding John Dawes before chipping the ball round JPR Williams.

The final try of the game was the epitome of what the Barbarians' rugby is all about. After a series of penetrating runs by David Duckham, Mike Gibson and Furgus Slattery, JPR Williams was on hand to carry

Gareth Edwards throws out a pass, with Phil Bennett pictured in the background.

the ball into the corner to seal the victory. Bennett converted to give the Baa Baas a 23-11 triumph over the All Blacks that everyone who attended the match will remember for the rest of their lives.

Barbarians team

1974 ALI V FOREMAN: RUMBLE IN THE JUNGLE

The "Rumble in the Jungle" was now-notorious promoter Don King's first event and he had persuaded both world champion George Foreman and former champion Muhammad Ali to separately sign contracts with him promising them a $5 million purse. As he didn't have that kind of money, he searched for a sponsor whom he readily found in Zaire's President Mobutu Sésé.

George Foreman was born in Texas on 10th January 1949 and, despite being in trouble with the authorities during his youth, qualified for the United States Olympic team by the age of 19. He went on to win the Heavyweight gold medal at the 1968 Olympic Games in Mexico City and turned professional the following year. His first fight at this level was a three-round demolition of Don Waldheim at New York's Madison Square Garden in June of that year and he went on to fight another dozen times before Christmas, with only two going the distance.

He got his title shot against the undefeated "Smokin'" Joe Frazier who had claimed the belt from Jimmy Ellis in February 1970 and successfully defended his crown on four occasions (including against Muhammad Ali in 1971). "Big George" at 6' 3½", floored the champion six times in just two rounds to stun the boxing world. Foreman himself retained his crown after beating Jose Roman and Ken Norton before facing Ali on 30th October 1974.

Ali had defended his title eight times since his rematch with Sonny Liston but he had been forced to fight abroad for the majority of these bouts because of his altercation with the US authorities. In 1964, Ali failed the qualifying tests for the Armed Forces but when these were revised two years later he became eligible to be drafted to Vietnam. He refused to go, stating he was a conscientious objector but was stripped of his title by the boxing commission in 1967 and sentenced to five years' imprisonment. He fought both counts and was eventually readmitted to the boxing fraternity in 1970 with the Supreme Court reversing his conviction the following year. Ali did, however, officially retire on 1st February 1970 to allow the winner of the upcoming Joe Frazier v Jimmy Ellis unification bout to be considered the undisputed champion.

Foreman and Ali spent much of the summer training in Zaire (now the Democratic Republic of Congo) to acclimatise themselves with the fight originally scheduled for September. A cut above Foreman's eye, however, delayed the bout by a month.

The contest started, on 30th October 1974, with the more agile Ali easily outmanoeuvring the bigger man as planned but the Louisville Lip soon found that he was tiring by moving quickly around the ring and that his punches – he landed nine heavy right-hand leads in the first round alone – were hardly having any effect on Foreman. As a result, he changed his tactics and decided to let Foreman expend his energy throwing punches at him that he could dodge or absorb as the moment saw fit. He labelled this strategy "rope-a-dope" and it soon became obvious that it was working.

Foreman – who had won 37 of his previous 40 fights by knockout with his last eight being finished by the

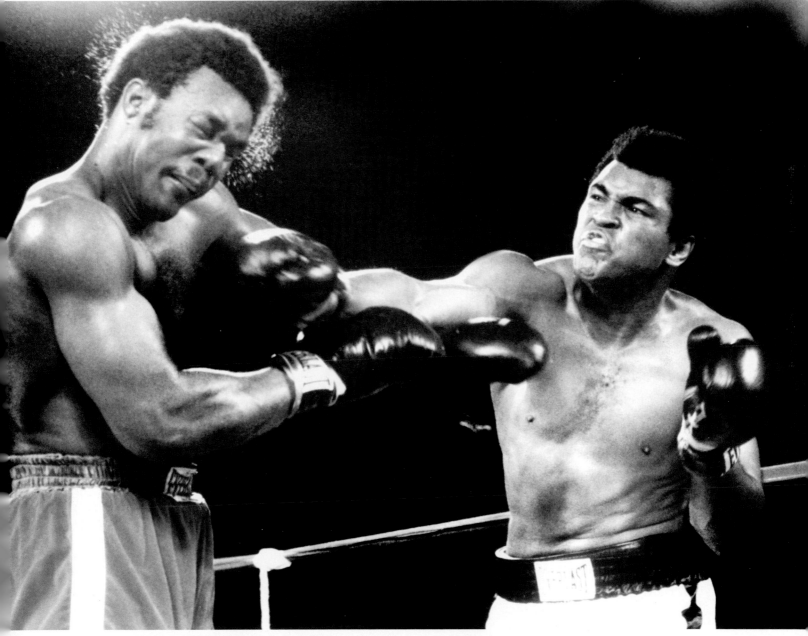

Muhammad Ali (R) flands a punch on George Foreman during the 'Rumble in the Jungle' match

second round – was looking visibly tired as the fight went on and his face was starting to show signs of the well-timed counter punches that Ali was able to land.

The challenger would also dupe his opponent into supporting his weight when they were in clinches, thereby forcing the champion to use up more precious energy in the stifling heat. He also taunted Foreman by telling him that his punches weren't hard enough.

As the fight drew on, the champion was rocked by Ali combinations in the fourth and fifth rounds but it was the left hook followed by a dynamite right in the eighth round that put an end to George Foreman's grip on the title. Foreman hit the deck but was slow regaining his feet and later suggested that he had been waiting for a signal from his corner that had come too late. In a huge upset, Ali had become only the second man – after Floyd Patterson – to regain the world heavyweight crown.

Many claim that this fight shows Ali – who went on to hold the title until losing to Leon Spinks in February 1978 – at perhaps his best, clearly demonstrating his ability to take a punch.

Foreman – who did not fight again until January 1976 – and Ali have since become firm friends and it was Big George who helped his former rival up to the stage when the documentary film of this fight, When We Were Kings, won the 1996 Academy Award for documentary feature.

Muhammad Ali, the three time heavyweight boxing champion, died at the age of 74. He had been fighting a respiratory illness. "The Greatest" was the dominant heavyweight boxer of the 1960s and 1970s, Ali won an Olympic gold medal in Rome in 1960, captured the professional world heavyweight championship on three separate occasions, and successfully defended his title 19 times.

Muhammad Ali training for the match in Zaire

Opposite: Muhammad Ali in action vs George Foreman

1975 WEST INDIES: 'ONE-DAY KINGS'- LORDS

5th January 1971 was the day when the first one-day international cricket match took place in Melbourne, as a gesture to ticket-holders when the first three days of the Ashes Tests were rained off. The authorities decided that, as a meaningful match was unachievable in the time remaining, it would be abandoned without a ball being bowled and a 40-overs-a-side match was hastily arranged.

After 46,000 people turned up for that game, one-day matches became an established feature of the international calendar and, in 1975, the World Cup of one-day cricket was inaugurated in England. To justify the event's billing as a world cup, a wider representation than the six Test countries was needed. A rather damp and squelchy qualifying tournament was held on club grounds in the Midlands, resulting in Sri Lanka and East Africa joining the major Test nations in two groups of four. South Africa were absent for political reasons.

The rain that dogged the preliminaries gave way to a hot, dry spell by the time the tournament got under way, so not a single minute was lost to the weather. The public were enthralled by the competition, and by the time the semi-finalists were known, the game was commanding attention not experienced for years.

The Ashes semi was played on a Headingley ground that was at its most helpful to seam bowlers. A green, used pitch and humid, overcast conditions caused the ball to swing and seam prodigiously. Australia's Ian Chappell put England in and Gary Gilmour bowled them out. At one time 37 for seven, England made a partial recovery to 93 all out. Australia, at 39 for six, were also

struggling, but Gilmour wielded his bat as effectively as he had bowled the ball, for 28 not out from as many balls to see Australia home by four wickets. In the other semi-final at the Oval, New Zealand reached 98 for one before suffering a spectacular collapse to be all out for 158. West Indies were 133 for one before a mini-collapse narrowed the margin of victory to five wickets.

The Lord's final was played on the longest day of the year, and needed to be, with the pulsating action lasting for all of 10 hours. Australia won the toss and fielded first, with immediate and spectacular results. Dennis Lillee induced the feisty little left-hander, Roy Fredericks, to tread on his wicket as he hooked him for six in the direction of St John's Wood Road. Gilmour and Jeff Thompson then took a wicket each to reduce West Indies to 50 for three in the 19th over.

That was when they struck back. Clive Lloyd joined Rohan Kanhai to add 149 in 26 overs. It was spectacular cricket between the imposing Lloyd and the diminutive Kanhai, causing bowlers to adjust their length just as the left-right hand combination required adjustment of line. Lloyd's hundred came from a mere 82 balls (the second 50 from 30 balls), and his side were in a strong position at the interval with 291 on the board.

Australia went after the target with a purpose. Although Rick McCosker went early, Alan Turner, Ian and Greg Chappell took the score along to 162 before Viv Richards completed his elimination of the trio with his third brilliant run out, exploiting indifferent running.

Keith Boyce had taken the first wicket and claimed three more, Lloyd himself chipped in to bowl Doug Walters, and Vanburn Holder ran out Max Walker to leave Australia facing defeat on 233 for nine.

The game appeared to be up, but Australia found the unlikely batting partnership of Lillee and Thomson edging them ever closer to their target. Fifty-nine were needed when they came together, but as so often happens in a seemingly lost cause, the pair began to enjoy themselves. Cheeky runs, the odd fortuitous edge and some thundering strokes of which any authentic batsman might be proud shook any complacency from the West Indians. Some of the world's leading bowlers were being treated with near contempt by two others, who happened to be batting at the time.

However, just as the notion of an outrageous victory was taking shape, the Australian reverie came to an end. Thomson had garnered 21 from as many balls when he was the fifth run out victim in the innings, leaving Lillee undefeated on 16. They had found the boundary just three times between them while putting on 41. The West Indies won the first World Cup final by a mere 18 runs, and as Lloyd accepted the trophy and the man-of-the-match award from Prince Philip, the doubting cricket establishment had to accept that the tournament had a permanent place in the game.

Greg Chappell avoids a bouncer, watched by Viv Richards (left), Australia v West Indies, 2nd Test, Perth, Dec 1975-76

Greenidge lbw Lillee, Australia v West Indies, 1st Test, Brisbane, November 1975-76

Cricket World Cup Final 1975 West Indies v Australia at Lord's

Ronnie Peterson (March-Ford) and Carlos Pace (Brabham-Alfa Romeo)
in the wet 1976 Japanese Grand Prix at Fuji

1976
JAPANESE GRAND
PRIX: FUJI

The 1976 Japanese Grand Prix on the Fuji circuit
marked the culmination of an incident-packed season
that had been peppered with excitement, innovation,
controversy and tragedy.

The year had started in a confused fashion. Hesketh
Racing announced their withdrawal from the sport citing
financial difficulties, only to return later in the year thanks
to a cash injection from newly found sponsors. Hunt,
jobless as the new season approached, was lucky to be

snapped up by the well respected McLaren team who had
just lost Emerson Fittipaldi – the driver having defected
to his brother's team in a decision that stunned the racing
world. The surprise of the Brazilian's move, however,
paled into insignificance with the sudden and tragic death
of racing legend Graham Hill whose life was lost along
with those of five of his Embassy team crew when his light
aircraft crashed on approach to Elstree Aerodrome.

McLaren had courted their first round of controversy at the hard fought Spanish Grand Prix held at the Jarama circuit on the outskirts of Madrid. Initially the result showed that Hunt had won with a margin of 31 seconds from Ferrari's Austrian superstar and championship leader Niki Lauda. However, scrutineering from FIA officials revealed the Briton's McLaren to be wider than permitted by the Formula One regulations of the time. Hunt was disqualified but was later reinstated on appeal although his team received a $3,000 fine for their trouble. A win for Hunt and a rare mechanical failure for Lauda's Ferrari at the French Grand Prix offered the first opportunity for the McLaren driver to close the point gap on the series leader.

McLaren hit the headlines for altogether different reasons as the championship was welcomed back to the British circuit of Brands Hatch. A first corner incident involving two Ferraris left Clay Regazzoni and Ligier's Jacques Laffite sidelined whilst Hunt's McLaren, forced airborne in the impact, suffered badly-damaged suspension. With the race red-flagged Regazzoni and Laffite prepared to restart in their spare cars. Hunt's mechanics, however, elected to quickly rebuild his car whilst officials argued about his eligibility to start. In the ensuing race Hunt finished victorious well over a minute clear of Lauda. Once again he was proclaimed winner but the objections soon came flooding in as it was claimed he should not have been allowed to take part after his car had received repairs. Initially the protests were rejected by the FIA but, under appeal from Ferrari, they were later upheld and Hunt was stripped of his win.

As the drivers arrived at a typically wet Nürburgring for the German Grand Prix concern was raised once more regarding course safety. This apprehension was proved valid when, on the first lap of the race, Lauda's Ferrari spun and hit a fence before bursting into flames and rebounding onto the track where it was hit first by Harald Ertl's Hesketh and then the Surtees of Brett Lunger. Hesketh's second driver, Guy Edwards, immediately stopped as did Williams's Arturo Merzario and the four drivers leapt to Lauda's aid – pulling him from the burning wreckage. There is no doubt that their actions save the Ferrari driver's life but, nevertheless, he was seriously burned and was rushed to Adenau hospital for emergency treatment. For a second successive Grand Prix the race was red-flagged and restarted and once again Hunt crossed the finish line in first place but fortunately this time there were no protests to register and the result stood.

With championship leader Niki Lauda hospitalised the series moved to the Osterreichring for the Austrian Grand Prix. Ferrari, still smarting from the events at Brands Hatch a month earlier decided not to race. Also absent from the grid was Formula 1 veteran Chris Amon who, having suffered two accidents already that season and witnessed the shocking incident at the Nürburgring, had decided to hang up his driving gloves for good. A fourth place for Hunt behind unlikely winner John Watson and a win at the following round in Holland signalled the start of his own personal drive for the title.

Monza witnessed the amazing return of Niki Lauda to Formula One. Bearing horrendous scars he was warmly welcomed back to the paddock by both drivers and fans alike. Proving that the events of The Ring had not dulled his ability he took a creditable fourth place whilst Hunt span out of contention to keep the Ferrari driver's title hopes alive.

Hunt's charge was revived as the championship moved across the Atlantic with wins in both Canada and at the Watkins Glen track in Upstate New York whilst Lauda, meanwhile, could only manage eighth and third places

James Hunt leads McLaren-Ford team-mate Jochen Mass in the wet 1976 Japanese Grand Prix at Fuji. In the background: Mount Fuji

respectively. In an incredible turn of events the two drivers were set to enter the final round at Japan's Fuji circuit separated by just three points.

Hunt once again caused controversy before the racing had even started when his McLaren team booked a private practice session on the Japanese track which had never before been used for Grand Prix racing but come qualification it was the John Player Team Lotus of America's Mario Andretti that took pole position ahead of the Briton by 0.03 seconds.

When race day arrived so did the weather – so much so that, following the Sunday morning free practice, cancellation looked likely with all the drivers complaining of severe aquaplaning and dangerous

conditions. Mindful of incidents earlier in the year the organisers were understandably worried. Even Hunt and Lauda both stated they would prefer not to race. A decision was taken to postpone the start from 1:30pm to 3pm in the hope of an improvement. After an additional delay of five minutes, the cars were away although barely able to see from one corner to the next.

Hunt pushed himself into an early lead ahead of Andretti and proceeded to quickly make ground on the Lotus. But then, with the race barely under way Lauda made a move that stunned everyone when he calmly peeled off of the racetrack and into the pit lane. Parking in his garage he climbed out of the car and said "It's just like murder out there, so I'm not going to do it".

He still knew that the championship was a possibility but it was now all down to Hunt. Signalled by his pit crew the Englishman began calculating what was required – a third place would guarantee him the title.

Pressing on in the appalling conditions everything looked to be under control until, on lap 20, the rains stopped and the track started to dry. As each lap passed his tyres began to struggle as their wet weather compound began to rapidly overheat. Disaster struck with just 12 laps remaining when his front left completely deflated. Diving into the pits, many, including the Ferrari mechanics, thought his

race to be over but the McLaren team rapidly fitted a fresh set of wets and sent him on his way again. Andretti was now in the lead followed by Depailler's Tyrrell, Regazzoni's Ferrari and the Surtees of Alan Jones with Hunt back in fifth. With just a handful of laps remaining it looked as if hopes of the Briton taking the title were fading but then beset by similar tyre problems, first Regazzoni and then Jones were forced to pit for fresh rubber. Hunt crossed the line in third place and as Britain's first World Champion since Graham Hill's triumph in 1968.

James Hunt (McLaren-Ford) in the wet 1976 Japanese Grand Prix at Fuji

1978
BEST EVER SCORE TO WIN THE MASTERS: GARY PLAYER

South African Gary Player has won 160 professional tournaments in his illustrious career and has travelled more than 14 million miles around the world. His achievements include 24 PGA Tour wins which span 20 years and more than 100 other non-senior golfing tournaments. He won the Australian Open seven times between 1958 and 1974 and has a total of 18 wins on the Australasian Tour between 1956 and 1981. Between 1955 and 1981, he clocked up 73 wins on the South African Tour (now called the Sunshine Tour) including victories at 13 South African Opens. He has won many Champions Tour trophies including three Senior PGA Tour Championships (1986, 1988 and 1990) along with the US Senior Open which he won on two occasions in 1987 and 1988. He also went on to win the Senior British Open three times in 1988, 1990 and 1997. However, his historic victory at the Masters in 1978 will be forever etched on the memory of the golfing world.

It would be the third Masters victory for Player and many were doubtful of his ability to achieve success at Augusta National Golf Club as he had been described as past his prime. He was really up against the competition in the final round but Player astounded the crowds when he orchestrated a miracle when his second shot at the 15th hole landed across the water and safely on the green with an eagle putt. He birdied the 9th, 10th and 13th holes to achieve a score of eight under par at the 15th. His excellent 80-foot putt took him within a comfortable distance of the hole. However it was a tricky putt that he safely delivered into the hole on the 15th to secure a joint first place position. It took him to the 16th hole with a score of nine under par.

By the 17th, hole he was 10 under par and needed an excellent putt to take him into the lead. It was the first time in the four-day tournament that he had a shot at victory and Player wasn't about to lose his focus. His putt on the 18th gave him a score of 64 for the round – it was a "course record" – one that still hasn't been equalled to this day. On the course to congratulate him was Seve Ballesteros. The birdie at the 18th hole and 11 under par had done it for Player with a final score of 64, 71, 78. The runners-up included Hubert Green, Watson and Funseth all at 10 under par.

The Masters Tournament, fondly known as the Masters, is the first in the season each year and unlike other major men's championships is only ever held in one place – Augusta National Golf Club. Designed by Bobby Jones and the great architect Alister MacKenzie, the course champions are automatically invited to play at the US Open, the Open and the PGA Championship

Gary Player at the US Masters, Augusta, Georgia, 1978

66

Gary Player lines up his putt during the 1978 Masters

for the following five years. Champions at Augusta are also invited to play at the Masters for life – although the field at this tournament is slightly smaller than most other majors with only around 90 players or so.

The tournament is held over four days and 72 holes and although the event follows the rules as set out by the United States Golf Association there are also special rulings at Augusta that are defined by the Masters Tournament Committee. As the field is relatively small for a golfing tournament it is traditional at the Masters for groups of three players to play the first 36 holes – usually over the Thursday and Friday – while a cut is then made once all players have participated in the first 36 holes. Another regulation of the Committee was that all players had to use the services of an Augusta National Club caddy although this was relaxed in 1983 and since then professionals have been eligible to use their own caddies.

The Masters originally began as the "Augusta National Invitational Tournament" at the insistence of a humble Bobby Jones, but in 1939 the legendary golfer relented and the tournament became known as the Masters

Tournament. The first Masters played the current holes from numbers 10 to 18 as the first nine while numbers one to nine were traditionally the second nine. Despite the common usage of the front and back nine, Augusta has tended to stick with the original choice of first and second nine when referring to the holes.

Controversy reigned in 2006 when the course was lengthened from 6,850 yards to 7,445 yards. The change drew fierce criticism from legendary players such as Jack Nicklaus, Arnold Palmer and Tiger Woods among others. However, three times Masters Champion Gary Player defended the changes. Player courted controversy himself with the golf club that actively discourages older players from participating in the Masters today. Player took no notice and challenged other competitors when he took part in the 2006 tournament at the age of 70.

Gary Player was the first non-US Master Champion in 1961 so it is perhaps fitting for this great sporting hero to hold the record of the lowest score on the course.

1980 FIVE NATIONS: ENGLAND

While England would prove to be the major force of the 1990s in the Five Nations, many took their 1980 Grand Slam success under captain Bill Beaumont to be the start of a golden era. Sadly, this was not the case as that proved to be their only title that decade, and having watched neighbouring Wales grab the limelight in the 1970s their fans were desperate for success.

England had been in the doldrums in the 1970s, failing to win a single game in 1972 and 1976 and winning just one game in 1974, 1975 and 1979. The 1972 season could not be completed due to the troubles in Ireland and the 1973 championship was shared between England, France, Ireland, Scotland and Wales as each of the five teams ended the campaign with two victories to their name.

The last match of the 1980 Five Nations tournament saw England travel to face Scotland at Murrayfield. Captain Bill Beaumont and his team knew that victory would mean England's first Five Nations championship since 1963, and their first Grand Slam since 1957.

John Beattie (centre) and his Scotland colleagues at the Five Nations

The campaign had begun well with a 24-9 victory over Ireland at Twickenham. Mike Slemen, Steve Smith and John Scott scored a try apiece with Dusty Hare adding three conversions and two penalties while Ireland could only reply with three penalties from Ollie Campbell. The other fixture of the opening weekend saw Wales beat France by 18-9.

England's second match of the season saw them travel to Parc des Princes to take on 1977 Grand Slam champions France. It was a much more closely fought encounter than England's previous fixture with both sides scoring two tries. France's came from captain Jean-Pierre Rives and Jean-Luc Averous while John Carleton and Nick Preston touched down for England. In the end, the difference between the two teams would prove to be kicking with Alain Caussade successfully slotting a conversion and a penalty through the posts. England, however, could rely on Dusty Hare (one penalty) and John Horton (two drop goals) to compete their scoring and claim a 17-13 triumph. In the other match, Ireland conquered Scotland by 22-15.

The following matchday paired England with Wales and it proved to be a very tight affair at Twickenham with England emerging 9-8 victors. Although the visitors scored the only two tries of the game through Elgan Rees and Jeff Squire, they had to play the last hour with 14 men after flanker Paul Ringer was sent off for a late tackle. Dusty Hare converted the last of his three penalty kicks in the dying minutes to dash Wales' hopes of a fifth consecutive Triple Crown. Ireland had the weekend off, as Scotland overcame France 22-14 at Murrayfield.

It was England's turn to watch the other games the following matchday and they would have been extremely happy with the results as, with Wales beating Scotland 17-6 and France edging out Ireland 19-18, it meant they went into their final match knowing they were already going to be crowned Five Nations champions. It just remained to be seen as to whether they could claim the Grand Slam as well.

As Ireland beat Wales 21-7 at Lansdowne Road, England were taking on the auld enemy, Scotland, for the 1980 Calcutta Cup. This cup had been presented to the RFU in 1878, having been crafted from silver that had been melted down from silver rupees owned by the now-defunct Calcutta Club in India. It was first played for the following year and, as the original is kept locked away in a vault, replicas are held by both the RFU and SRU.

The match turned out to be a classic with England unstoppable in the first half. In his first international season, young centre Clive Woodward was really making a name for himself. He ran rings around the Scots and set up the first two tries for Carleton and Slemen which Hare duly converted. A scrum in the corner seemed to be heading over Scotland's goal-line when Scott and Smith contrived to give Carleton the opportunity to score his second try of the game. Three penalties followed before half-time, two to Scotland's Irvine and one to Hare, giving England a 19-3 lead.

Just eight minutes after the restart, Smith scored his side's fourth try and, as the second half drew on, it looked like the hosts could pull themselves back into the game but it was not to be. Despite Rutherford and Tomes registering tries for Scotland, Carleton completed his hat-trick and England won by 30-18 to claim their first Grand Slam in 23 years.

Beaumont's heroes remain the only English side to ever win the Grand Slam on Scottish soil, an accomplishment made much sweeter by the fact it was won against their fiercest rivals.

John Beattie in action for Scotland

1980
SUGAR RAY LEONARD
V ROBERTO DURAN

Two of the greatest fighters the world has ever seen clashed twice during the year of 1980. "Sugar" Ray Leonard and Roberto Duran entertained the boxing audiences with two spectacular clashes for the WBC Welterweight title in June 1980 at Montreal's Olympic Stadium and then five months later at the Superdome in New Orleans.

Sugar Ray Leonard – born on 17th May 1956 in North Carolina – first won his title against Wilfred Benitez in November 1979 before defending it in a fourth-round knockout of Dave "Boy" Green four months later.

Roberto Duran was born on 16th June 1951 in Panama and won his first professional fight in February 1968 with a unanimous decision over Carlos Mendoza. He had previously won both the WBA and WBC Lightweight belts and came into this fight with just one loss in 73 bouts.

In the first encounter, the Panamanian started strongly and soon landed an overhand right in the second round that began the damage. He followed this up with a left hook to Leonard's body and then a right that sent the champion into the ropes. The next two rounds saw Duran continue to dominate, scoring massive punches with his left hooks and overhand rights.

Leonard was allowing Duran to box in close quarters, something his corner had wanted to avoid, but the champion did come back into the contest in the fifth round when he started to find his range with his left hook. He, like his opponent, concentrated on body shots aimed at weakening the other boxer but it was Duran who was enjoyed the majority of the scoring.

Leonard's corner implored him to stop trying to guess what his opponent would do and get his punches in first and in the later rounds he did try this strategy. The 13th proved to be the most exciting of the night, with Duran targeting Leonard's body with a fierce right to the body that forced the champion to drop his arms to fend off the next blow. Unfortunately for him, the next blow was a left hook to his head. The champion recovered to land a left hook of his own among other punches which saw Duran on the ropes this time.

Roberto Duran raises his arms in defeat as Sugar Ray Leonard wins the fight in the 8th round and becomes the new welterweight champion

Both fighters appeared tired in the final two rounds and each would have been glad to hear the final bell. Duran was the happier of the two when the referee announced the judges' unanimous verdict: 144-145, 147-148, 144-146.

While Leonard could at least console himself with the biggest payday in sporting history at $10 million, the boxer with the normally silky skills had lost his title to the brawler from Panama and he wanted revenge. He would only have to wait five months for his chance.

The rematch turned into something of a farce when Duran pulled up with two minutes and 44 seconds of the eighth round gone and conceded the fight. He later attributed his decision to the stomach cramps that he claimed he had been suffering since round five but then went on to state "I've gotten tired of the sport. I feel it's time for me to retire."

The spectacular had commenced with Ray Charles – after whom Leonard was named – singing "America The Beautiful" but then the hostilities began in earnest. Leonard controlled the first two rounds with consummate ease, landing telling left hooks, right hands and beautifully timed combinations that shook Duran. The champion tried to utilise the same tactics that had won him the first fight and for a while in the third round it looked like it was working but Leonard was wise to this strategy and quickly moved away from the ropes to give himself space to work.

Although he showed no outward signs of any discomfort, Duran was beginning to suffer from alleged stomach

Sugar Ray Leonard victorious, after Roberto Duran quit with 16 seconds left in round 8 at Louisiana Superdome

cramps in round five but by the end of the sixth round he is supposed to have told his interpreter that his arms were getting weak. Leonard was in total control of the seventh round, landing punch after punch and even beginning to taunt his opponent. And then it was all over, Duran saying to the referee "No más, no más!" (the Spanish for "no more").

An hour after the fight, the Louisiana State Athletic Commission announced it was withholding the Panamanian's share of the money pending an examination but a week later a flu-ridden Duran appeared live on television to withdraw his decision to retire.

He later won Light Middleweight and Middleweight world titles and fought Leonard for the WBC Super Middleweight belt in 1989 (losing a unanimous decision) before finally retiring in 2001 at the age of 50. Leonard himself went on to win Light Middleweight, Middleweight, Super Middleweight and Light Heavyweight titles before retiring in 1997.

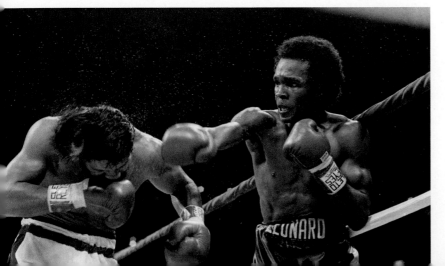

Leonard sends the perspiration flying as he hits Roberto Duran with a hard right hand during the 6th round of their Welterweight Championship fight

1984
PORTUGUESE GRAND PRIX: ESTORIL

There is an old adage spoken time and time again that reminds competitors that, in the race for a championship title, every point counts. Never more has this rung true than the stunning climax of the 1984 World Drivers' Championship held on the Portuguese circuit of Estoril late in October. It had been another season punctuated by incident and controversy not least that surrounding the rain-soaked Monaco Grand Prix.

Rain had fallen steadily on the Monte Carlo circuit for most of the day resulting in a delay to the start of 45 minutes. No sooner had the field got away than the

first incident of the day occurred when the Renaults of Derek Warwick and Patrick Tambay collided on the entry to the first corner – the latter of the two drivers suffering a broken leg in the impact. As the race progressed Alain Prost took control in his McLaren closely pursued by the Lotus of Briton Nigel Mansell whilst Niki Lauda in the other McLaren chased in third. To the delight of his legion of fans Mansell took the lead on lap 11 only to crash heavily into the pit wall just five laps later leaving the McLarens in first and second place. Carving his way through the field was a young driver called Ayrton Senna competing in his first year of Formula 1 – having started in 13th place he was already up to third and closing fast on Lauda. By lap 19 he was ahead of the Austrian whose luck ran out five laps later as he spun on the wet surface and crashed heavily into the barriers at Casino. Closing on Prost at a rate of 1.5 seconds per laps the Brazilian looked unstoppable but even more stunning were the efforts of German newcomer Stefan Bellof who, after starting at the back of the grid, was now himself reeling in both of the frontrunners.

As each lap passed and with the wolves at his door, Prost was seen gesturing to the clerk of the course in an attempt to have the race stopped. Then, after just 31 laps and without warning, the red flags appeared and Prost was declared victor. Both Senna and Bellof were incensed feeling rightly that they had both been robbed of a fair chance of victory. With the race having failed to reach half distance, only half of the available points were allocated – Prost taking just 4½ for his trouble instead of the usual 9. This decision would prove critical to one driver's success and another's failure in Portugal.

Lauda arrived at Estoril as championship leader with 5 wins and 66 points to his name. In second was his team mate, Alain Prost, who, despite having taken 7 victories that season, was 3½ points in arrears thanks to the Austrian's ability to constantly score well at each round. To be assured the world title, all Lauda had to achieve was a first or second place. For Prost it was a little more complicated – he had to win and Lauda had to finish no higher than third.

Early dampness in qualification gave way to a warm and drying track that saw Nelson Piquet place his Brabham at the front of the grid alongside Prost's McLaren with the Toleman of Senna and Rosberg's Williams filling row two ahead of the black and gold

JPS Lotuses of de Angelis and Mansell. Suffering from turbo problems Lauda could only manage to qualify on the sixth row back in 11th position. His work was cut out.

Piquet's qualifying excellence came to nothing when, as the lights changed, he completely messed up his start and rocketed from pole position to lantern rouge within a handful of seconds. Rosberg was quick to capitalise on the Brazilian's misfortune and soon took control ahead of a charging Mansell, Prost and Senna. As the cars entered their second lap Prost moved up on Mansell and into second place whilst Lauda, starting his long and torturous climb through the field slipped past American Eddie Cheever into 10th. Eight laps later and Prost was in the lead – there was no denying the determination of the man to become France's first world champion!

Ahead of Lauda, a battle had developed between Michele Alboreto, Elio de Angelis, Derik Warwick and Stefan Johansson. The Austrian champion-in-waiting, more than aware that often the better part of valour is discretion, decided to sit tight and watch rather than unnecessarily throw himself into the fray. His experience paid dividends when in the following laps both Warwick and Alboreto spun and de Angelis dropped back with tyre problems. Lauda was up to sixth but, meanwhile, Mansell had passed Rosberg for second. For Lauda it was time to attack and a lap later he made a move on Johansson – one so tight that he broke off the front wing of the Swede's Toleman Hart. After seven more laps he was hot on the tail of the battling Rosberg and Senna but these two appeared as nothing more than a minor distraction to the thundering McLaren and both were swept aside with ease.

Prost, however, was still in the driving seat for the title. After 35 laps of racing, he led Mansell by a comfortable 10 seconds with Lauda a further 30 seconds back and failing to close. Fifteen laps later Prost looked unstoppable; his lead had increased to 20 seconds with Lauda failing to make inroads into his advantage but his good fortune was about to run out. Mansell, still pushing hard in second, was unaware that his brake fluid was leaking until, on lap 52 he spun. Recovering quickly he was back into the action before Lauda had a chance to pass him but the Austrian had closed the gap down to a few feet. One lap later his brakes failed again and another spin ensued. Lauda was past and into second. There was nothing more Prost could do. He backed off a little to save his car in case Lauda should fail to finish but it was already a fait accompli.

Prost may have crossed the line as winner of the 1984 Portuguese Grand Prix but it was Niki Lauda, finishing in second place, who was World Drivers' Champion. And what was his margin of victory? One-half of a point.

Niki Lauda at the 1984 Portuguese Grand Prix

Nelson Piquet of Brazil drives the #1 MRD International Parmalat Brabham BT53 BMW S4 turbo during the Portuguese Grand Prix

1984 OLYMPICS: LOS ANGELES

Los Angeles was the only city prepared to bid for the right to host the 1984 Games, other nations having been deterred by the terrorist actions of the Munich Games and the financial debacle of those in Montreal. For the first time since 1896, the Games became dependent on the financial support of corporate sponsorship as significant federal funding was not made available. Unwittingly these games would set the blueprint for future Olympics.

Unsurprisingly, considering the US led boycott of the Moscow Games, the Soviet Union declined their invitation to attend citing anti-communist demonstrations in the USA and a worry for the safety of their athletes as the reason. Compared to the 65 nations that had rejected their invitations to the 1980 Olympics, only 14 declined to attend the 1984 Games in support of the USSR. This number may seem small but these nations accounted for 58% of the gold medals awarded at the 1976 Montreal Games. In total, a record 140 nations were represented at the 1984 Olympics.

In winning gold medals in the men's 100m, 200m, long jump and the 4x100m relay 23 year old American Carl Lewis not only delighted the thoroughly partisan crowd but also matched the 1936 achievement of his hero, Jesse Owens. 1976 400m hurdles gold medallist Edwin Moses won the event for the second time having missed out in 1980 due to the western boycott.

The Los Angeles games would see a number of Olympic firsts for female athletes. American Joan Benoit won the first women's marathon with her compatriot, Connie Carpenter-Phinney, winning the inaugural women's cycling road race. Other events to be added included women's rhythmic gymnastics and synchronised swimming.

Controversy surrounded the final of the women's 3000m as barefoot British athlete Zola Budd collided with favourite Mary Decker of the USA, bringing her to the ground. Although it was apparent that Decker was largely at fault it was Budd who would feel the wrath of the nationalist American public.

German Ulrike Meyfarth had set a record at the 1972 Games in winning the high jump and becoming the youngest winner of an individual track and field event. In 1984, she again won that title becoming the oldest ever winner of the event.

In the rowing a young and little known Steve Redgrave representing Great Britain won his first Olympic gold medal giving spectators a taste of what was to come over the next 16 years.

Left to right: US athletes Thomas Jefferson, Carl Lewis and Kirk Baptiste at the final of the Men's 200 Metres at Los Angeles Memorial Coliseum, during the Olympic Games, Los Angeles, 8th August 1984. They won the bronze, gold and silver medals, respectively. Lewis set a new Olympic record of 19.8 seconds

From left to right: Carl Lewis crossing the line to win the final of the Men's 4 x 100 metres relay at the Los Angeles Memorial; Lewis during the race; Lewis takes a victory lap after winning the Gold Medal in the men's 100 m

Carl Lewis

Born in Birmingham, Alabama, in the summer of 1961 the son of two athletics coaches, Carl Lewis grew up in New Jersey taking to athletics as a teenager. His first Olympic selection was short lived with the United States team boycotting the Moscow Games of 1980. Lewis had wait for the Los Angeles Olympics in 1984 to make an impact.

Having achieved victory in the 100 metres, long jump and 4x100 metres at the 1983 World Championships Lewis was considered a favourite for success in Los Angeles. His goal was to emulate his hero, Jesse Owens, by winning all three plus the 200 metres. This he did with ease setting new world 4x100 metres and Olympic 200 metres records in the process.

Hoping to repeat this performance at the 1998 Seoul Games, he won the 100 metres following the disqualification of Canadian Ben Johnson but suffered a surprise defeat in the 200 metres by fellow countryman Joe DeLoach. The US 4x100 metres team was then disqualified in the heats. As a consolation he easily defended his long jump title.

Defending his long jump crown at the 1992 Barcelona Games Lewis found himself pushed close by compatriot Michael Powell. Despite this he retained his title by a narrow margin to win his third Olympic long jump title. Running the anchor leg of the 4x100 metres Lewis secured another gold medal and yet another world record.

Returning to the Olympics in Atlanta he was not expected to make an impact having barely qualified at the US Olympic trials. Proving the doubters wrong Lewis put in a massive 8.50 metres leap to secure his ninth Olympic gold medal. An achievement shared by only three other athletes.

1985
EUROPE CLAIM RYDER CUP

Battling it out since 1926, the British and Irish team (who became the European Tour team in 1985 – although players from other nations were included from 1979) and the US have enjoyed peaks and troughs throughout the history of the Ryder Cup. The year of 1985 – with Seve Ballesteros having been coaxed back into the team two years previously by captain Tony Jacklin – was to see the US lose the trophy for the first time since 1957.

The US team, hoping to defend their nine victories since 1959, could have been forgiven for thinking that the result was a sure thing. But the hard work put in by the European team was about to render the US team disappointed for the first time in 28 years. In 1957 the British and Irish team pulled off an unlikely victory in the Ryder Cup when Christie O'Connor drove off the tee on the final day for the home side at Lindrick in Ireland. The team under the captaincy of Dai Rees were not given much of a chance of beating the dominant US team. Great Britain and Eire started the singles 3-1 down. However the Americans found the pace too hot at Lindrick and their opponents – who included the likes of Peter Mills playing in his first Ryder Cup match – were playing like champions. In the singles matches the US only won one of their games – all the rest went to the challengers.

In 1985, European captain Tony Jacklin insisted on preparation and professionalism from team members – something that was to stand them in good stead. The team effort was paramount and went on to produce one of the most memorable images in golfing history. The score was 13-8 to the European team, courtesy of Paul Way, as Sam Torrance took to the green elsewhere for a short putt that could produce a birdie and win the hole. Torrance was triumphant when he achieved just that on the 17th hole. He followed it with a huge drive down the fairway in pursuit of the 18th hole and waited patiently while his opponent took his shot. Torrance only needed one more to win the trophy. Andy North's tee shot found the lake and the anxious faces of the US spectators were plain to see. Sam Torrance prepared himself to shoot the ball over the water at the 18th. A comfortable shot saw him make the green with only a few feet between the ball and victory. Torrance made history when the ball found the hole with just one putt. Jacklin, the European team and their supporters were elated. After 28 years the Europeans had finally done it. It was to pave the way for more exciting Ryder Cups to come.

Two years later saw the European team in the States where they retained their crown thanks to the likes of Seve Ballesteros and Jose Maria Olazabal. These two sporting giants, along with the rest of the team, were to lay the foundations for a 15-13 win. It was pinned on Larry Nelson at the 18th hole who needed to somehow win the hole in order for the US to have a realistic chance of winning the trophy back again. Nelson's decisive chip from the rough just short of the green was clean and smooth, but just not powerful enough and the ball landed a little to one side of the cup. The final putt came from Seve Ballesteros who stood up from collecting his ball from the hole looking ecstatic.

The home crowd were as pleased for the visitors as the supporters that had travelled from Europe.
It was a successful tournament for the European team who had started to even the balance of power with a consecutive win.

The European team were triumphant once again in 2002 when the Ryder Cup was hosted at the Belfry. Harrington took the European team three up with a birdie putt at the end of the front nine. Colin Montgomerie continued the trend when he bagged a possible four out of five points at the end of his round at the 14th hole. Team members Langer, Harrington, Bjorn and Fasth all looked good after day one and it was incumbent on the Americans to step up their pace. Phil Price made a promising start against Phil Mickelson. However he struggled at the 395 par four

6th hole while Mickelson made it all look so easy landing comfortably on the green. Price struck back and landed neatly just yards from the hole. Harrington meanwhile on the par three 14th hole needed a putt to win his match. He duly delivered and the home side were progressing well. Langer faced the same situation as Harrington when he reached the par five hole at the 15th. Like Harrington he won the match. However, it wasn't all easy on the fairways and many of the players on both teams found some moments difficult. Westwood conceded defeat to American Verplank on the 17th green while Mickelson was eventually beaten by Price. The Americans still trailed two points behind when the score reached 12½ to 10½. The match ended 15½ to 12½.

Ryder Cup European team

1986 AUSTRALIAN GRAND PRIX: ADELAIDE

For the second year running, the culmination of the Grand Prix season was scheduled to take place in Australia. Despite a long and illustrious history of producing some of the world's best drivers it was only after 35 years of competition that the nation had finally been granted its own race. Air travel was faster and more economic and TV coverage guaranteed global exposure. Like Monaco and Long Beach, the Adelaide track, based around the city's Victoria Park, was a tight and twisting street circuit of the old-school full of thunderingly fast straights, 90 degree turns and stop-go switchbacks.

With just this one round left to run, Nigel Mansell was leading the Drivers' Championship on 70 points with a tally of 5 wins but he had far from dominated the season. Hot on the Briton's heels with 63 points to his name was his Williams-Honda team mate Brazilian Nelson Piquet whilst just a single point further in arrears was reigning champion Alain Prost of the McLaren team. The prospect of three drivers being in with a chance of the title had the journalists and pundits reaching for their calculators and working out the possible permutations.

With a seven-point advantage and only nine points on offer for a win there was no doubt that Mansell was the hot favourite. This was reinforced in qualification when the man from Surrey put his Williams FW11 on pole position with a time of 1:18.403. However, joining him on the front row was Piquet whilst Prost was just a row behind – separated on the timing sheets from the frontrunners by a remarkable performance by Ayrton Senna in an underpowered Lotus 98T.

Charging away from the grid surrounded by a shower of sparks from the titanium skid plates fitted to the cars of the era and with the Drivers' title firmly in his sights Mansell could not have done worse. Heading into the second corner he was forced to yield to Senna who, although well out of the running for championship glory, was determined as ever to place himself on the top step of the podium. Mansell then found himself being passed first by the Williams of his team mate and next by Keke Rosberg's Tag-McLaren. Now in second place Piquet decided that he was not in the mood for hanging about and immediately attacked Senna's lead. Making good use of his superior power he was quickly through, becoming third race leader with less than one 2.35 mile lap covered.

As the cars stormed along the Adelaide street circuits pit straight for the second time Rosberg moved swiftly ahead of Senna. Mansell, meanwhile, was still running in fourth place but after another two laps he too sped past the underpowered Lotus to move up to third – a position which could not only secure him a place on the podium but also the title. Another two laps passed before Prost, also contending title honours, moved ahead of Senna. The shuffling, however, was far from over. Just one more lap into the race and Rosberg attacked for the lead. As his tyres struggled for grip he slid his McLaren inside the Williams to take control of the race.

Opposite: Alain Prost celebrates winning the Fosters Australian Grand Prix on 26th October 1986

The winner at Adelaide the year before and also having victories at Monaco and Detroit in his palmares, Rosberg was a past master on tight street circuits. Putting his expertise to good use, he was soon pulling away from the rest of the field. On lap 23, Piquet instantly demoted himself from a steady second to fourth place behind Mansell and Prost with a spectacular spin. Prost's advantage over the Brazilian was, however, short lived when four laps later he punctured and was forced to pull in for fresh rubber. Quick work by his mechanics meant that he was able to rejoin in fourth place but for all those watching his hopes of a championship title did not look good.

Following his spinning antics Piquet had the bit grasped firmly between his teeth. With each lap that passed he gradually ate into Mansell's advantage until, on lap 44, they were together. Knowing that a third place would secure the championship Mansell reluctantly let him through and in to second. Prost was also pulling back lost ground and on lap 57 made contact with the other two title contenders. They were now running like a train in second, third and fourth but the advantage was still with the Englishman.

Rosberg's substantial lead looked secure until lap 63 when his tyre de-laminated throwing chunks

of rubber into the air. Unable to continue there was nothing he could do but park his beleaguered McLaren at the trackside and spectate. Promoted to second place, the situation now looked even better for Mansell. With Ayrton Senna having retired with engine problems there was a considerable gap back to Stefan Johansson's Ferrari in fourth. All he needed to do was finish in the top three and Prost and Piquet's positions would be irrelevant.

Then it happened; one of the most iconic moments in motor racing history. With his Williams travelling at over 180mph Mansell's left rear tyre exploded sending debris and sparks everywhere. Fighting hard for control he unbelievably managed to steer the crippled machine towards an escape road and to safety. In an instant, his championship hopes were over.

Fearing that the problems that had caused him to crash might also affect the second Williams, Piquet was quickly brought into the pits for new tyres. Rejoining in second place the Brazilian tried bravely to regain lost ground but it was to be in vain when, after 82 laps of hard racing, Alain Prost crossed the finish line as winner of the Australian Grand Prix and 1986 World Drivers' Champion.

Alain Prost drives the Marlboro McLaren International McLaren MP4/2C TAG V8 turbo during the Australian Grand Prix

1987 NICK FALDO WINS THE OPEN

Home to the Honourable Company of Edinburgh Golfers, Muirfield is the oldest golf club in the world, founded in 1744. The course is hugely demanding and its dangers are obvious. The top golfers have long considered Muirfield to be a fair test of ability in championship golf and so perhaps it is fitting that Nick Faldo should win the Open here in 1987. Faldo managed to par all 18 holes in his final round at the tournament to secure his first Open victory.

Muirfield is a 6,801-yard par 70 course and like all the courses at Gullane is hilly with characteristic heather and gorse. There are also demanding downhill holes that require a focused mind – although these are more like those to be found on an inland course rather than a links course. Muirfield, like many other famous links (and inland courses), was designed by Old Tom Morris and the current course opened in 1891. The course has played host to the Open Championship on 15 occasions, the last time in 2002, when Ernie Els won his first Open victory.

Back to 1987 and Faldo set out to claim his first Open Championship on the final day. It wasn't to be all plain sailing though and his third shot at the 17th saw his ball roll down a hilly bank and into the edge of the rough by the green. The putt didn't have quite enough power behind it and the ball swung away from the hole on the sloping green. Faldo at this point was five under par and in second place behind Paul Azinger who was six under par at the 16th hole but the American's lead was

only a slender one stroke ahead. Faldo meanwhile was struggling to get a birdie. Although he had had several chances to achieve a birdie, he just hadn't managed to. The weather was more a hindrance than a help and by the time Faldo reached the 17th hole, a thick mist hung over Muirfield threatening to envelop the tournament.

Faldo's drive from the 18th tee was impressive but what also helped was that Azinger's tee shot from the 17th ended up in a small but deep bunker. His only choice was to get the ball out sideways which he managed comfortably. With only 195 yards to go, Faldo produced an excellent shot onto the 18th green. Azinger's third shot to the 17th landed around 100 yards from the green. His fourth shot produced much better results and his ball sat safely on the 17th green. Faldo meanwhile missed a birdie on the 18th green and overshot the hole by quite a long way. By now Azinger was five under par at the 17th. Faldo shot the 18th in four leaving Azinger needing a four to tie at the 18th or a three to win the championship. Azinger failed on both counts and Faldo became the new Open Champion – his first ever.

Born on 18th July 1957 in Welwyn Garden City, Faldo originally worked as a carpet fitter and played amateur golf – he borrowed a set of clubs from his next-door neighbours to begin with – winning the British Amateur Championship and the British Youth Championship both in 1975.

Nick Faldo with the Open Championship trophy after his win by one shot over Paul Azinger and Rodger Davis

The following year he turned professional and gained success relatively quickly by finishing in eighth position on the European Tour order of merit in 1977 and in third place a year later. In each season he won a European Tour event and also in 1977 he was the youngest player to participate in the Ryder Cup at the age of 21. He became a leading player in the 1980s after he remodelled his swing to give him a better chance at the major tournaments. By 1987, Faldo was a strong contender and the change in swing gave him his first shot at a major championship – the Open at Muirfield – in which he claimed victory.

After his first championship during the late 1980s and throughout the entire decade to follow, Faldo was the number one golfing hero in the world. He remained calm and composed under pressure and had a canny knack of intimidating his opponents which made him hard to beat. He went on to win the Masters Tournament at Augusta National Golf Club in 1989 and then again in 1990. He again won the Open Championship in that same year and then again for the third time in 1992. Faldo twice made the number one slot on the order of merit list for the European Tour in 1983 and 1992 while his earnings of more than £1.5 million that year broke all existing records.

He continued as a European Tour player and spent time in the US before deciding to concentrate his career with the PGA Tour in a bid to win further major championships. As three of these, the Masters, the US Amateur and the US Open are all held in the States it became impossible for Faldo to dedicate himself to the European Tour. The gamble paid off and Faldo claimed his sixth – and final championship – at the Masters in 1996.

Nick Faldo, Open Champion, with wife Gill and baby daughter Natalie

1990 WIMBLEDON: MARTINA NAVRATILOVA

Martina Navratilova, during her reign at Wimbledon, achieved a total of nine singles titles. Six of these were won in consecutive years, from 1982. Up to this point, Navratilova had already proved herself by raising the women's game to a new standard. She did this with a combination of power, competitiveness and aggression, previously unseen in female tennis. The woman who declared that "Wimbledon is like a drug. Once you win it for the first time you feel you've just got to do it again and again and again" won her first title in 1978 against Chris Evert, who she beat again 12 months later.

Thus began a series of wins at the All-England club, with few interruptions, until 1988. During this time, Navratilova became the new dominating figure in women's tennis. Her Wimbledon wins were most often against her most formidable opponent, Chris Evert. The last of these was in 1985. Steffi Graf finally broke Navratilova's run at the top, becoming the first person to beat Navratilova in a Wimbledon singles final in 1988. This win was repeated in 1989. However, Navratilova was not yet to be written off. She reached her ninth successive final in 1990, at the age of 33. She was now all set up to face Zina Garrison on Centre Court.

"There were no glitches this time; everything came up nines," said Navratilova. She had been helped by a twist of fortune: Garrison's win in the semi-final against Graf. This had the effect of knocking a serious threat out for Navratilova. Graf was fast becoming the new force in the women's game. She was now the player to beat. "It would have been more fitting to play Steffi, but at the same time, obviously Zina earned her place there," said Navratilova. "The event overtakes the person you end up beating."

Navratilova showed her pleasure in this turn of events by demonstrating her still formidable powers in a two-set display of prowess. "I wanted the record, no doubt about it," Navratilova told the Telegraph much later. "I was lucky enough to set a few records in my career, but they just happened because I played well for a long time, but when I realised I was in with a chance of breaking the Wimbledon singles record, it became a big goal of mine."

However, Navratilova was determined not to be overwhelmed by the momentous event until she had succeeded fully, remaining steely and focused throughout the match. Now 33 years old, she knew that she couldn't take anything for granted. In the event, she was to produce one of the most accomplished and controlled performances of her long career.

Garrison made a good start, as she held to love in the opening game and then earned a break point in the second. But Navratilova found her pace and saved the game with a volley into the corner. She then won the game after the third deuce and then immediately broke serve, giving her the confidence and a psychological advantage.

Navratilova held her serve comfortably to take the set 6-4. She then broke Garrison in the third game of the second set. All of which meant that the champion was now fully in command. After saving a break point in the next game it seemed there was no problem or challenge that could halt her progress, as she wrapped up the championship in an hour and 15 minutes.

In the end, Navratilova played more elegantly and intelligently than Garrison, defeating the 26-year-old Texan, 6-4, 6-1, in the 75-minute final. "She was a step ahead of me the whole time," said Garrison after the event. Navratilova celebrated her victory by climbing up into her box and hugging coach Craig Kardon and Billie Jean King.

The following year, Navratilova defeated Graf in their last major tournament match, in the semifinals of the 1991 US Open, ending a historic grand slam rivalry 5-4 up. Navratilova would go on to reach one more Wimbledon final in 1994 but was beaten by Conchita Martinez. She later said: "[1990] was a lovely way to finish the story, if you like. A golden day."

Navratilova kisses the trophy after winning the Ladies Singles Final at Wimbledon

Martina Navratilova of Czechoslovakia reacts against Zina Garrison-Jackson during the finals of the women's singles at the Wimbledon Lawn Tennis Championships 7th July 1990

Journey to greatness

Martina Navratilova was born in Prague, Czechoslovakia. Her parents divorced when she was three, and her mother moved the family to Venice. Martina took the surname of her stepfather. When she was eight, her father committed suicide.

Navratilova had already started to play tennis regularly when she was seven. Watching Wimbledon on television as a child, she had no idea how long the grass would be, imagining it to be a couple of inches long like a football pitch. Eventually, she would see it up close for herself.

Early in her career, she set about challenging herself with objectives for devastating fitness levels and commitment. In 1972, at the age of 15, the left-hander won the Czechoslovakia National Tennis Championship. A year later, she made her debut on the US Lawn Tennis Association professional tour, but did not turn professional until 1975. Her first professional singles title was achieved in Orlando, Florida in 1974, when she was still only 17.

Her life was about to take another momentous step. An 18-year-old Navratilova went to the offices of the Immigration and Naturalization Service in New York in 1975 and notified them that she wanted to defect from communist Czechoslovakia. Within a month, she received a green card and, in 1981, became a fully naturalized US citizen.

Navratilova took her collection of Wimbledon titles to a staggering 20, in 2003, after victory in the mixed doubles. She shares that achievement with Billie-Jean King. She retired in 1994, the year she lost in her last final singles tournament appearance against Conchita Martinez, although later returned to play doubles matches.

Navratilova remains the most successful female tennis player of the open era, amassing an unmatched number of professional records over the course of a career that spanned an incredible four decades. Along the way, she won a staggering 59 grand slam titles, including a record nine Wimbledon singles championships. She also remains a role model for women around the world. "I think the key is for women to not set any limits," she said.

Opposite: Martina Navratilova serves against Zina Garrison-Jackson
during the finals of the women's singles at Wimbledon

1993 THE BALL OF THE CENTURY: OLD TRAFFORD

"The first couple of balls you bowl are just warm-ups, and you just hope to get them somewhere near the right spot. To bowl the perfect leg-break first up – I think it was just meant to be." So said Shane Warne of the delivery that became one of the most talked about ever. Modest though his assessment may seem, it should be added that Warne was never the sort of bowler to eschew risk at the start of a new spell.

He was 23 and had been playing Test cricket for little more than a year. A solitary wicket for 228 runs in his first two Tests against India had hardly hinted at anything exceptional, and an invitation followed from Rod Marsh to return to the Australian Cricket Academy, which he had left under a cloud a couple of years earlier. Under the tutelage of Terry Jenner, Warne gave up beer and lost some weight. Recalled in Sri Lanka, he was trusted by his captain, Allan Border, to bowl in the closing stages of a tight encounter in Colombo. Warne took three for 11 in five overs as Sri Lanka fell 16 runs short. An epic journey had begun in earnest.

Such was the impression he made on the next two series – he took seven in an innings against the West Indies and 17 in three Tests in New Zealand – Warne came into the 1993 Ashes encounter with no less a batsman than Martin Crowe canvassing him as the best leg spinner in the world. Australia expected their opening attack of Craig McDermott and Merv Hughes to spearhead their defence, but they also knew of England's historic frailty against leg spin, apparent against Pakistan's Abdul Qadir a decade earlier.

Knowing Warne a little by reputation but not at first hand, England nonetheless went into the first Test reassured by the ample presence in their middle order of Mike Gatting, an acknowledged expert at playing spin. But they had to wait until day two to face Warne, because Graham Gooch gave Australia initial use of the Old Trafford pitch. It did not reap early rewards; Australia's opening pair of Mark Taylor and Michael Slater posted 128 before being parted. At stumps on day one Australia were 242 for five, and Warne opted to settle his inaugural Ashes nerves by spending the evening with Hughes, his all-or-nothing Victorian team-mate.

Given the opening stand, England did well to dismiss the tourists for 289 on day two, with the off spin of Peter Such significantly accounting for six wickets. Gooch and Mike Atherton gave England a solid start, and after Gatting got off the mark with a boundary, Warne came on to bowl the 28th over of the innings.

Shane Warne of Australia with his Man of the Match award after the 1st Test match between England and Australia at Old Trafford

England batsman Robin Smith is bowled by Shane Warne during the 1st Test match between England and Australia at Old Trafford in Manchester, 3rd June 1993. Australia won by 179 runs

His first ball in Ashes cricket emerged from the back of his hand, initially appearing to be on course for Gatting's pads. As the batsman later recalled: "He put so much spin on it that the ball swerved just before pitching, even wider of the leg stump. I thought I had it covered, but it turned past my bat – and everything else I had behind it – and just clipped the off bail. If it hadn't, it would have been Ian Healy who looked stupid rather than me, as he was waiting to take it down the leg side."

Such was his scepticism about whether such a delivery was geometrically possible, Gatting stood for a moment before confirming with the square leg umpire, Ken Palmer, that he was out. The ball had done more than just dismiss him; it had set the tone for the entire series, and indeed for more than a decade. Australia's confidence rocketed; England's was fatally undermined. Robin Smith was soon caught at slip off a barely inferior delivery from Warne, who then induced Gooch, the only England batsman to play him with any confidence, to hit a full toss to mid on. England eventually subsided to 210 all out, and lost the match by 179 runs.

Warne was to strike 34 times in the 1993 Ashes series, and England were no nearer mastering him on his final tour of England 12 years later, when he took a record 40 wickets despite Australia's defeat. Can one delivery ever have played such an influential part in the outcome of a rubber? Warne himself wrote later: "Psychologically, I think, we had struck a massive blow for the rest of the series and none of the batsmen really tried to get after me. As for being the 'ball of the century', I don't think that can be for anyone to say. So much of cricket's rich history has gone unfilmed." True enough, but no one watching was able to suggest another contender.

1993 EUROPEAN GRAND PRIX: DONINGTON PARK

When the Formula 1 circus arrived at Donington Park for the third round of the 1993 World Championship, it was the first time that the premier motor racing class had graced the Derbyshire circuit since 1938. On that occasion, it was the Tazio Nuvolari who reigned supreme in the conquering Auto-Union Type D – the original Silver Arrows. The 1993 race proved to be no less exciting, as once again a single driver dominated proceedings in what is held to be one of the greatest Grand Prix performances in the history of the sport.

Alain Prost had won the opening round of the championship under clear skies at South Africa's high altitude Kylami track. He had demonstrated that, in no uncertain terms, the Williams-Renault was the car to beat. But the applecart had been upset just a fortnight later when, in a chaotic race held in atrocious conditions, Ayrton Senna had taken victory, the 100th for McLaren, whilst Prost had squandered his pole position advantage having crashed on lap 29.

Prost was back on the front of the grid at Donington. Alongside him was his team mate Damon Hill who was competing in his second Formula 1 season having just joined to replace Nigel Mansell who had decided to try his hand in the US Indy Car series. Heading up the second row was another relative newcomer to the sport – Michael Schumacher – who was enjoying his second full season with Benetton-Ford. To his side was championship leader Ayrton Senna.

Ayrton Senna takes the lead from Alain Prost on the first lap of the 1993 European Grand Prix at Donington Park

Weather conditions for race day morning were appalling. It was obvious that all of the cars would need to start on wet tyres but for how long? Wet weather tyres are designed purely for use in the rain relying, as they do, on the standing water to cool the special soft compound grooved rubber. Using them on a dry track would cause rapid deterioration risking handling problems, blowouts or worse.

As the lights changed from red to green and the field accelerated towards Redgate, Prost and Hill made their predictably good start. Senna, meanwhile, found himself boxed in behind the Karl Wendlinger. Wendlinger's charge continued and before the first corner he was also ahead of Schumacher. Senna, however, was about to launch a stunning attack.

By the time the cars were exiting Redgate he was already in front of Schumacher. Then, heading down through the perilous Craner Curves he was up alongside Wendlinger before moving ahead on

the entry to the Old Hairpin. Charging up the hill under Starkey's Bridge he rapidly closed in on an unsuspecting Damon Hill before making his move up the inside of the British driver at McLeans. Prost was now in his sights as the cars stormed along Starkey's Straight and through the Esses. Approaching the Melbourne Hairpin he moved alongside and then, as the cars turned in, he forced his way through once more and into the lead. Senna immediately started to stretch out a lead. At the end of the second lap he already had a 4.25 second advantage over Prost and within another lap this was extended to almost 7 seconds.

Conditions changed on lap 7 when the sun started to shine and a dry line became visible. First to pit for slick tyres was Ligier's Martin Brundle but his tactics proved rather premature when he spun his car in the damp on his out lap and was forced to retire.

Michael Schumacher and K.Wendlinger at the Sauber Ilmor 1993 Euro GP at Donington

Hill, running in third place pitted on lap 10 followed by Senna and then Prost. Senna was quickly back out on track, this time on slick tyres, and continued to defend a lead of about five seconds.

By lap 20, he was already catching backmarkers when the rain once more started to fall heavily on the track. Hoping to gain some advantage Prost was quick to pit for a fresh set of wets whilst on track both Schumacher and Mark Blundell spun off. Hill chose to pit on lap 23 but Senna just kept on going on slick rubber – incredibly posting faster lap times than his wet-shod opponents. Satisfied that he had gained enough advantage he eventually came in for new tyres still managing to rejoin the fray in first place after the stop with 15 seconds in hand.

Once more the track started to dry and on lap 31 Prost was in for another pit stop and fresh slicks. This time Senna chose to pit at the same time but

an uncharacteristic slow change by his McLaren mechanics saw him rejoin the action behind Prost. But this would only last for four laps as again the heavens opened and the Frenchman charged into the pits for wets on lap 35.

With slicks still fitted to his car, Senna stayed out regardless, setting faster and faster lap times against all odds. Ten laps on and the track started to dry yet again. Prost attempted his sixth change of tyres but disaster struck when, hurrying to get back into the action, he stalled his McLaren. Wasting valuable seconds as the mechanics attempted to re-start his car, he could do nothing but watch as his Brazilian rival sped past his stranded car to lap him.

Having at last decided to change to new slicks, Senna headed into the pits but as he did so spots of rain started to fall. Waving at his mechanics he continued to drive straight through and back onto the track having lost little time in the process. Hill was now closing at three seconds per lap allowing the Briton to un-lap himself with just 10 laps remaining. On lap 66 Senna went in for his final set of wets. Rejoining well ahead there was nothing the field could do to stop him speeding on to victory with only Damon Hill finishing on the same lap. Rubens Barrichello had managed to move up to third place following Prost's dreadful pit stop but the unfortunate Brazilian's hopes of his first podium finish were dashed when his fuelling system malfunctioned with just two laps remaining.

Senna's astounding victory had seen him out-drive his opponents in the most amazing demonstration of wet weather driving since Jackie Stewart's astounding Nürburgring drive back in 1968.

Michael Schumacher at the 1993 Euro GP

Ayrton Senna in McLaren MP4-8 1993, at the European Grand Prix at Donington

Heinz-Harald Frentzen at, Nürburgring, Germany, 1995

1995 EUROPEAN GRAND PRIX: NÜRBURGRING

By 1995 the days of the full 14 mile Nordschleife with its 100 treacherous bends twisting their way through Germany's Eifel Mountains were long in the past. The ultimate drivers' circuit had last been used for a Formula 1 race back in 1976 after which the German Grand Prix had switched location to the infinitely safer but somewhat sterile Hockenheimring. A shorter 2.8 mile Nürburgring circuit, the GP-Strecke, was, however, completed in 1984 and had since become a regular home for the Grand Prix of Europe. Although it paled in comparison to its legendary predecessor it was a state of the art modern circuit built wholly with the safety of both drivers and spectators in mind.

The 1995 championship had been brought to life by a fantastic battle for supremacy between Benetton's controversial German ace Michael Schumacher and Williams's home-bred hero Damon Hill. Schumacher had undoubtedly dominated proceedings having already taken six victories to Hill's three within the first 13 rounds of the competition but the war of attrition that raged between the two drivers had kept fans on the edge of their seats and sparked countless debates over the merits of each driver's sometimes unconventional methods and tactics.

Qualification for the European Grand Prix had seen Hill pipped to the post by his Williams team mate, David Coulthard, who was riding on a wave of self-confidence having taken top honours over Schumacher in Estoril just a week before. Schumacher was, therefore, relegated to the second row of the grid alongside Ferrari's Gerhard Berger whilst Jordan's Eddie Irvine and Jean Alesi in the second of the Prancing Horses filled the third.

Heavy rain had battered the GP-Strecke on the morning of the race and, although the showers had ceased long before the start, most of the teams elected to take to the grid on full wets. Only Ferrari and McLaren were exceptions to the rule opting for slick tyres and dry weather suspension and wing settings in the hope of the quick formation of a dry racing line.

David Coulthard's getaway from the grid was exceptional as was Schumacher's – the German slipping comfortably into second place by the time the field reached the first corner as Hill, starting off of the racing line, struggled for grip on the wet and greasy tarmac. As expected, both Ferraris dropped back through the field as did the McLarens – the difference being that although Alesi and Berger were relegated to sixth and ninth respectively McLaren's Mika Hakkinen and Mark Blundell found themselves being passed by all and sundry before taking up positions as honorary back markers.

Ferrari's tactics started to pay off as the race approached its 12th lap – a dry line was forming and Maranello's best were starting to make progress through the field. First to fall was Schumacher's Benetton team mate Jonny Herbert, next was the Jordan of Eddie Irvine. The charging Alesi was already up to fourth place before being catapulted into a 20 second lead as Coulthard, Schumacher and Hill headed into the pits for slick rubber and a splash of fuel.

Race winner Michael Schumacher, Jean Alesi and David Coulthard celebrate on the podium after the European GP 1995, Nürburgring, Germany

Once out of the pits, Hill immediately started to attack Schumacher – his car obviously faster with fresh tyres and a full fuel load. Unsurprisingly Schumacher was not in the mood to capitulate. Making his car as wide as possible and holding defensive lines into every corner it seemed impossible for the popular Briton to make a move past the German master. Trying a little too hard, Damon was forced to lock his wheels to avoid a collision on more than one occasion but he would not give up. Giving Schumacher a taste of his own ruthless medicine, he forced his way ahead and into third place but soon lost his hard-fought advantage – almost spinning at the final corner to allow his rival the opportunity to effortlessly slip past. This time, Schumacher seized his chance to pull away.

Ahead, Coulthard was starting to experience problems of his own as the heavy fuel load upset the handling of his car – the Scot having been forced to start in his spare car following an incident in the pre-race warm-up lap. Schumacher wasted no time in bearing down on the second Williams and was quick to pass the ailing FW17 – his move duplicated by the chasing Hill just a single lap later.

Alesi, meanwhile, continued to press on ahead with his lead now extended to a healthy 30 seconds and half distance approaching. Diving into the pits for his scheduled tyre and fuel stop he rejoined with Hill close on his tail – Schumacher having elected to make his stop at the same time. Recognising that he had an opportunity to distance the German, Hill chose to attack Alesi but, in an ill-timed attempt at passing he damaged his nose cone and was forced to pit on the next lap.

Schumacher, meanwhile, had decided that a safe second place was not good enough and started to post lap after blistering lap at breakneck speed to gradually reel in Alesi's wayward Ferrari. Each time he passed the finish line the margin was slashed yet again.

Mika Hakkinen with McLaren team boss Ron Dennis, team manager Jo Ramirez, Steve Nichols (right) and Mika's race engineer on the grid, Nürburgring

Hill too was keen to make up for lost time but he paid for his over-exuberance with a heavy crash into the barriers and was forced to retire.

With just three laps remaining Alesi's mirrors were filled with the sight of Schumacher's blue and yellow Benetton until, approaching the tight left-right chicane, the German made his move. Running audaciously fast into the corner he forced his way inside Alesi's car. With their wheels overlapping and perilously close to making contact there was nothing the Frenchman could do but surrender his position. Schumacher was through and on his way to his seventh victory of the season and his second World Drivers' Championship.

1996 SRI LANKA WIN WORLD CUP: LAHORE

England had been the venue for the first three World Cup tournaments. In 1987 the event was split between India and Pakistan, with another dual hosting arrangement in 1992 as matches were played in both Australia and New Zealand. In 1996, this went a stage further with a tripartite agreement featuring India, Pakistan and Sri Lanka. Of these, either India or Pakistan might have been fancied to become the first host nation to win the cup, while at least one of the hosts could reasonably have been expected to reach the final. One of the hosts did, but nobody predicted that instead of either Mohammad Azharuddin or Wasim Akram lifting the trophy, the honour would fall to a somewhat rotund 32-year-old by the name of Arjuna Ranatunga, who hailed from Sri Lanka.

India had caused a major upset in an earlier tournament by beating the then mighty West Indies in the 1983 final at Lord's, but India was an established cricketing nation and Sri Lanka were relative newcomers to the big league. The country had experience of playing one-day cricket in previous World Cups and ICC Trophy events, but it was not until 1982 that they played their first Test match. In the blink of an eye, in international cricket terms, they had gone from new boys to world champions.

Their path to the final in Lahore was strewn with obstacles, although they put such inconveniences to good use. Australia and the West Indies refused to go to Sri Lanka to play scheduled matches because of civil strife in the country, so the Sri Lankan players remained fresher than some. The boycott scarcely affected Australian or West Indian chances of progression, because three minnows had been included in the 1996 tournament. Of these, Kenya, pulled off one of the greatest upsets of all time by beating the West Indies, but were later eliminated along with Holland, the United Arab Emirates and Zimbabwe. So, the newly introduced quarter-final stage of the World Cup included all the major countries.

Sri Lanka had developed a new approach to the limited-overs game. Rather than waiting for the final 10 overs for an all-out assault, as was the accepted strategy in one-day cricket, Sanath Jayasuriya and Romesh Kaluwitharana blitzed the attack for the first 15 overs while the fielding restrictions were in force.

Aravinda de Silva reaches 100 at the World Cup Final 1996
Australia v Sri Lanka at Lahore

Aravinda de Silva batting against Shane Warne

England, to their surprise, fell foul of this strategy in the quarter-finals, while India beat Pakistan, West Indies defeated the fancied South Africans and Australia accounted for New Zealand.

Australia overcame the West Indies by five runs in one semi-final in Chandigarh, as the men from the Caribbean lost their last eight wickets for 37 runs. If that was dramatic it was nothing compared with the other semi-final in Calcutta, where Sri Lanka made 251 for eight before India collapsed to 120 for eight in 34.1 overs. It caused an explosion of unrest in the stands and the match was called off, forfeited by India.

So to the final in Lahore, the first day/night international to be held in Pakistan. Ranatunga won the toss and took the unusual step of putting Australia in. The previous five finals had been won by the side batting first, and Australia would have taken that option due to an uncharacteristic lack of attention to detail. They had only practiced during the day, whereas Sri Lanka had gone to the Gaddafi Stadium to experience the lights. It was then that they encountered the heavy dew prevalent at the time and coach Dav Whatmore, in consultation with the captain and senior lieutenants, decided to avoid being in the field as the turf, and the ball, became saturated.

By the 27th over of their innings Australia were cruising towards a substantial total, with only one wicket down and 137 on the board. That a star-studded batting line-up should then be restricted to 241 for seven says much for the perseverance of the Sri Lankans. So did the way they set about chasing the runs. The openers failed for once, but Asanka Gurusinha (65) and Aravinda de Silva, with an undefeated and perfectly paced 107, put on 125 for the third wicket. Ranatunga himself tickled the winning runs through the off side to reach 47 not out, and Sri Lanka had won a sensational victory by seven wickets with 22 balls to spare.

The rain was just beginning to fall as Ranatunga stepped forward to receive the silver trophy. As he did so, a new cricketing power emerged and as he held the spoils aloft, a war-torn country was sent into raptures of delight that continued long into that, and many another, night.

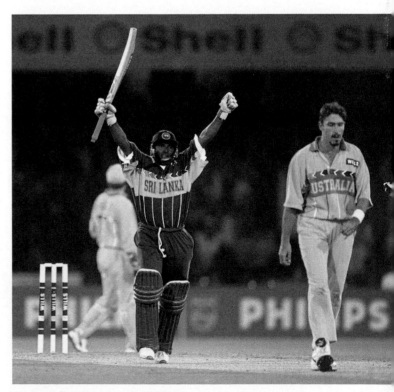

Aravinda de Silva celebrates his achievement

1997 TIGER WOODS WINS THE MASTERS

It must have seemed like a miracle when rookie Tiger Woods pulled off a 12-stroke lead to win the Masters Tournament in 1997 in his first professional event. No one was surprised when he reclaimed Augusta for the US in record-breaking fashion at the tournament a year after turning professional. His sponsors were so confident in his success that they had already paid him $60 million when he turned professional in August 1996. He won the tournament 18 under par. His closest rival was Tom Kite at six under par. His stunning performance was remarkable.

Tiger Woods has golf in his blood. He began playing at the age of two and quickly became a child prodigy. At the age of three, he putted with Bob Hope in a television appearance on The Mike Douglas Show and at the same age shot a score of 48 over nine holes at the Navy Golf Club in Cypress, California. Born on 30 December 1975 in Cypress, Eldrick Woods was nicknamed "Tiger" after a friend of his father who served with him in Vietnam. He is the youngest of his father's four children and the only child from his father's marriage to his mother Kultida. He first appeared in Golf Digest aged five and went on to win the boys' category in the 9-10 age group at the Junior World Championships – he was only eight years old. He won the championship six times in all including four consecutive wins between 1988 and 1991.

By the age of 15, he became the youngest US Junior Amateur Champion in golf's history which he successfully defended in 1992. Also in 1992 Woods entered and competed in his first PGA Tour event at the Los Angeles Open. Then in 1993 he won his third consecutive US Junior Amateur Championship. The following year was to see Woods become the youngest US Amateur Champion. His outstanding career grew from strength to strength and the awards and accolades are too numerous to mention. The year 1995 saw Woods as the only amateur to make the cut and to appear in the Masters where he tied in 41st place. Then in 1996 aged just 20 he went on to become the first golfer in the history of the sport to win three consecutive US Amateur titles. His first professional tournament was the Greater Milwaukee Open and despite tying in 60th place he won other tournaments and qualified for the Tour Championship. In his first year as a professional he was named as 1996's "Sportsman of the Year" by Sports Illustrated and Rookie of the Year by the PGA Tour.

His influence on golf has been monumental and his impact, particularly in the US, unique. His record win at the Masters in 1997 made him the youngest ever winner of the major tournament and the first winner of African/Asian descent. He set 20 Masters records and tied six further records which has led him to become the most prolific golfer in the world – perhaps the most prolific golfer in the history of the game.

Opposite: Tiger Woods poses with the Masters Trophy after finishing 18 under par to win the 1997 Masters at the Augusta National Golf Club, 13th April. Wood is the youngest player to ever win the tournament

In less than a year of being a professional, the young player from California was named the number one golfer in the Official World Golf Rankings – he holds the record for getting to the top slot in just 42 weeks. But Woods' fortunes turned the following year when he only won one PGA Tour event. Woods himself put it down to the changes he was making in his swing. Like great golfers before him changes in style take time and effort and often result in a lack of previous form before a new breed of player is unleashed.

By June 1999, Woods was back – as predicted – on top form and his win at the Memorial tournament perhaps marked the beginning of what was to become a prolonged period of dominance in the world of golf. He achieved 17 wins at PGA tournaments over 24 months and went on to claim a further 32 victories over the next five seasons. By the end of the 1990s, Woods was a phenomenon and ended the 1999 season with eight convincing wins. He became the PGA Tour Player of the Year and remained in the top 10 of the Official World Golf Rankings for 264 consecutive weeks.

Woods also proved himself a record-breaker when he beat Old Tom Morris's score of 1862 to win the biggest victory margin in a major championship when he won the 2000 US Open at Pebble Beach with a 15-stroke lead. That year also saw Woods in exceptional form, he began the season with a fifth consecutive victory and he won the Open on the Old Course at St Andrews with a convincing eight-stroke win. The mighty player also set a new record when he completed the course in the lowest ever score in a major championship finishing 19 under par. With his Open victory came another accolade – Woods became the youngest ever player to achieve a Grand Slam.

Opposite: Tiger Woods during the first round of the 1997 Masters Tournament

1998 WORLD CUP: FRANCE V BRAZIL

France were one of the early runners in the race to host the 1998 World Cup finals, announcing their intention to submit an application in 1988, a good ten years before the tournament was due to take place. Their eventual selection, which would coincide with the sixtieth anniversary of the only other occasion they had hosted the finals, was duly ratified in 1992.

Across the globe in South America, the nine teams entered into the competition (Brazil qualified as holders) were put into a single League for the first time, with each side facing the others home and away, with the top four qualifying for the finals.

Brazil as holders kicked off the finals on 10th June and were soon off the mark, opening the scoring after just four minutes against Scotland.

There was a sending off in the next second round match, that which pitted England against Argentina, in what was undoubtedly the game of the round. There have been countless column inches devoted to the incident that saw David Beckham sent off early in the second half, equally divided between those who felt England would have won had he remained on the field, others bemoaning the fact that Diego Simeone, who Beckham half-heartedly lashed out at, conned the referee and got away virtually blameless. For long spells, England played better than their opponents, despite the man disadvantage, and although there was no further score in either the second half or extra time, England could point to a disallowed goal from Sol Campbell that was perhaps a decision even harsher than that which saw Beckham dismissed. England

went out once again on penalties.

The final quarter-final place was claimed by Croatia, rapidly becoming the dark horses of the competition, with Davor Suker, ultimately to claim the Golden Boot, netting the only goal of the game from the penalty spot.

On the same day, Argentina slipped out of the competition, eventually beaten by a piece of sublime skill by Dennis Bergkamp that saw him control a 60-yard pass with his first touch, elude his marker with his second and fire home at the near post with his third, as the game entered its final minutes. Earlier Patrick Kluivert had given Holland the lead on 12 minutes, only for Claudio Lopez to level the score six minutes later. Then came 70 minutes of stalemate, the game only enlivened by Ortega's dismissal two minutes from time. With extra time looking a certainty and the game calling out for a moment of inspiration to settle the tie, up stepped Dennis Bergkamp.

Holland hoped for more of the same in the semi-final against Brazil, but Bergkamp was kept quiet, only finding the net in the penalty shoot out. Brazil were also somewhat subdued, taking the lead through Ronaldo a minute after the restart for the second half and lacking punch up front for the rest of the game. With three minutes to go and Brazil staring the final

France were one of the early runners in the race to host the 1998 World Cup finals, announcing their intention to submit an application in 1988, a good ten years before the tournament was due to take place. Their eventual selection, which would coincide with the

France team celebrate winning Brazil v France 12th July 1998

sixtieth anniversary of the only other occasion they had hosted the finals, was duly ratified in 1992.

Across the globe in South America, the nine teams entered into the competition (Brazil qualified as holders) were put into a single League for the first time, with each side facing the others home and away, with the top four qualifying for the finals.

Brazil as holders kicked off the finals on 10th June and were soon off the mark, opening the scoring after just four minutes against Scotland.

There was a sending off in the next second round match, that which pitted England against Argentina, in what was undoubtedly the game of the round. There have been

countless column inches devoted to the incident that saw David Beckham sent off early in the second half, equally divided between those who felt England would have won had he remained on the field, others bemoaning the fact that Diego Simeone, who Beckham half-heartedly lashed out at, conned the referee and got away virtually blameless. For long spells England played better than their opponents, despite the man disadvantage, and although there was no further score in either the second half or extra time, England could point to a disallowed goal from Sol Campbell that was perhaps a decision even harsher than that which saw Beckham dismissed. England went out once again on penalties.

Brazil fans before the final Brazil v France 12 July 1998

The final quarter-final place was claimed by Croatia, rapidly becoming the dark horses of the competition, with Davor Suker, ultimately to claim the Golden Boot, netting the only goal of the game from the penalty spot.

On the same day Argentina slipped out of the competition, eventually beaten by a piece of sublime skill by Dennis Bergkamp that saw him control a 60-yard pass with his first touch, elude his marker with his second and fire home at the near post with his third, as the game entered its final minutes. Earlier Patrick Kluivert had given Holland the lead on 12 minutes, only for Claudio Lopez to level the score six minutes later. Then came 70 minutes of stalemate, the game only enlivened by Ortega's dismissal two minutes from time. With extra time looking a certainty and the game

calling out for a moment of inspiration to settle the tie, up stepped Dennis Bergkamp.

Holland hoped for more of the same in the semi-final against Brazil, but Bergkamp was kept quiet, only finding the net in the penalty shoot out. Brazil were also somewhat subdued, taking the lead through Ronaldo a minute after the restart for the second half and lacking punch up front for the rest of the game. With three minutes to go and Brazil staring the final in the face, Kluivert came to Holland's rescue with an equaliser. With no further goals in extra time the game moved into a penalty shoot out, the third and thankfully last of this particular competition. Claudio Taffarel saved Cocu and Ronald De Boer's efforts to eventually give Brazil a 4-2 win and a place in the final.

Croatia set about proving their victory over Germany in the quarter-final had been no fluke by taking the game to France in their semi-final clash. Suker put the Croatians ahead a minute after half time, stunning the partisan French crowd, but a minute later Lilian Thuram levelled the score. Roared on by the crowd and strengthened by the introduction of Thierry Henry and David Trezeguet, France began to take control and, 20 minutes from the end, Thuram netted his and France's second goal. The sending off of Laurent Blanc four minutes later put the pressure back on France, but the ten men held out to make the final.

Davor Suker had one more goal in his locker, his sixth of the tournament and the eventual winner in the third and fourth place play-off against Holland, Robert Prosinecki giving Croatia the lead only for Boudewijn Zenden to level eight minutes later. Prosinecki's goal was historic, allowing him to become the first player to score in World Cup finals for two different nations, having previously found the net for Yugoslavia in 1990.

If David Beckham's dismissal attracted intense media interest, at least as far as the English were concerned, then it was nothing compared to the comings and goings surrounding the Brazilian camp before and after the World Cup final. Sometime during the night, on the eve of the final, Ronaldo, something of a talisman for the Brazilians, announced himself unwell, suffering a fit, according to some sources. He was rushed to hospital and, irrespective of the outcome of the tests conducted on the player, coach Mario Zagalo decided to omit him from the team for the match. Depending on which source you choose to believe, either Ronaldo made a miraculous recovery (unlikely, given the performance he was to put in on the day) or team sponsors Nike insisted he be reinstated, Ronaldo was named in the starting line-up for the final.

He was not alone in not performing on the day, with only Dunga emerging from the final on the Brazilian side with any sense of at least sustaining his reputation. The rest were as much off the pace as Ronaldo, and Zidane, atoning for his earlier indiscretions, netted twice with headers to put France in the driving seat. As much as they huffed and puffed, Brazil had little or no answer and were seldom in the game once France were two goals ahead. Even the French temporarily pushing the self destruct button, with Marcel Desailly getting himself sent off on 68 minutes, did not inspire or ignite Brazil. In the final moments Emmanuel Petit netted a third, the 1000th goal France had scored in the competition.

Despite their disciplinary record, which saw them have three players sent off in the competition, France were just about worthy winners, aided as they were by the inept performance of the Brazilians at the final stage. Their flamboyancy may have won them fans aplenty in 1982 and 1986 but it had not won them the trophy (although they did collect the European Championship in 1984). A solid and tougher approach may have lost them fans, at least outside their own country, but it did result in them winning the trophy which they were largely instrumental in getting off the ground. Funny old game, as some might say.

France were not the only ones to suffer from disciplinary problems, with a new record of twenty-two red cards being issued, along with 257 of the yellow variety, almost four a game! That it was the likes of Zidane, Beckham and Kluivert who should see red did not present the game in the best possible light but try telling that to countless Frenchmen. Seventy years after the World Cup was brought into being and French sculptor Abel Lafleur had presented his design to FIFA, his countrymen had finally got their hands on its successor.

2000 BELGIAN GRAND PRIX: SPA FRANCORCHAMPS

Despite having won more rounds of the 2000 World Drivers' Championship than any other competitor, Ferrari's Michael Schumacher was not leading the race for the title as the series arrived at the Belgian circuit of Spa Franco champs. That honour was held by McLaren's Mika Hakkinen who, with three wins and five second-place finishes to his name, led the German by two points. Waiting in the wings just a further four points in arrears was Hakkinen's square-jawed Scottish team mate David Coulthard who had also achieved three wins within the opening 13 rounds.

With qualification held under beautifully clear skies, Mika Hakkinen took his fifth pole position of the year with an advantage of almost 0.8 seconds over second-placed Jarno Trulli with Jenson Button, racing in his first season of Formula 1, and Michael Schumacher filling the second row. However, the Finn had benefited from a clear, traffic-free lap whilst the majority of the field, including the other championship frontrunners, had had to contend with waved yellow flags at the bus-stop chicane which undoubtedly had taken the edge off their performances. Hakkinen conceded that his advantage was not as great as it seemed and that the race would be hard fought from start to finish.

In the early hours of Sunday morning, the day of the race, it started to rain very hard and by dawn the heavy showers had been joined by a rising mist that sat low over the undulating circuit. It was still raining as the drivers set out for their free practice session. Lapping in the atrocious conditions at over 13 seconds slower than the previous day it was a grim reminder to the drivers of just how difficult a circuit Spa is to

master. When it bites it bites hard as was found out by Giancarlo Fisichella who was lucky to emerge unscathed from the wreckage of his Benetton after crashing heavily into the Armco at the Stavelot curve.

By the time the race was due to start, the rains had ceased but the track was still perilously wet and the decision was taken to invoke a rolling start. As the safety car switched off its flashing lights and headed into the pits Hakkinen was away and making good use of the clear track ahead and the confusion thrown up from the dense spray enveloping the field behind. Meanwhile, Michael Schumacher moved ahead of Button at the chicane after the Briton got out of line in a brave attempt to pass Trulli's Jordan. By the next corner Schumacher was ahead of Trulli. Once more Button attempted the pass but this time he made contact sending the luckless Italian into a spin and out of the race. Button recovered to resume in fifth having gifted third to his team mate Ralf Schumacher.

After five laps, a dry line was starting to form and the sun was shining brightly. Hakkinen had extended his lead to 10 seconds as the first of the cars, Jean Alesi's Prost-Peugeot, headed into the pits to change to slicks. A lap later and Schumacher was also running on fresh rubber and on lap seven Hakkinen made the inevitable stop.

It was soon clear to those watching that Schumacher's dry setup was far better than that of Hakkinen's McLaren and he began to close the gap on the flying Finn. Hakkinen responded well but on lap 13 made an unforced error by touching a wet curb at

Stavelot and putting his car into a spin. Remarkably, he managed to control his high-speed skid but, having briefly ended up on the grass, his five second advantage over Schumacher was instantly converted to a five seconds deficit.

On lap 22 and now 11 seconds ahead of Hakkinen, Schumacher made the second of his scheduled pit stops. Five laps later the McLaren also headed in. With new tyres and a quick tweak of the front wing, Hakkinen sped back out onto the track but now, thanks to the efforts of his mechanics, he was just seven seconds behind and starting to close in. Lap after lap the gap was reduced until, with just four circuits remaining, Hakkinen was running deep in Schumacher's slipstream.

Powering out of L'Eau Rouge Hakkinen made his move. Closing fast down the back straight he started to sweep inside Schumacher but the German was not willing to give in that easily and swept across to close the door on his opponent – the cars just inches apart at over 300 kmh. Hakkinen immediately regrouped himself and prepared to try again.

Once again, it was L'Eau Rouge that provided the springboard but this time as Schumacher and Hakkinen charged along the back straight there was something new to contend with – they were about to lap the BAR of Ricardo Zonta. Schumacher waited until the last possible moment before swinging out to overtake in another attempt to close the door on his rival but Hakkinen had a plan of his own and dived up the inside of Zonta and into the lead.

Three laps later, Schumacher had to settle for a valiant second place whilst victory went to a deserving Hakkinen after one of the bravest and most spectacular overtakes in motor racing history which even Schumacher conceded was "an outstanding manoeuvre".

Ralf Schumacher (L) sprays champagne on Mika Hakkinen (C) and German Michael Schumacher (R) at the end of the Belgian Formula One Grand Prix in Francorchamps

Michael Schumacher (L) drives his Ferrari ahead of McLaren driver David Coulthard

Jenson Button goes past Jarno Trulli

2002

LEWIS V TYSON

After all the hype and bravado, this fight turned out to be more of a one-sided battle than many thought possible. When the fight was announced in January 2002, "Iron" Mike Tyson and Lennox "The Lion" Lewis had to be pulled apart. Indeed, Tyson was forced to pay his opponent $335,000 out of his fight purse for biting him at the press conference.

The organisers were not taking any chances on hostilities, which began earlier than scheduled, when the fight did eventually take place on 8th June, with a dozen or so security guards in the ring with orders to keep the boxers apart until the first bell. Several states – as well as the boxing mecca of Las Vegas – had refused Tyson a licence in view of his sordid history but Memphis bid $12 million to win the right to stage the fight that was eventually held at the Pyramid.

Lewis – born on 2 September 1965 and holder of the WBC, IBF and IBO Heavyweight titles – went into the fight with a 40-2-1 record (31 knockouts) while Tyson's read 49-4, 2 no contests (43 knockouts) but he had the physical advantage at 6' 5" tall, an 84" reach and weighing 246¼lbs. Bear in mind that Tyson (30 June 1966) stood at only 5' 10", had a 71" reach and weighed in at 234 lbs.

The opening round proved to be a cagey affair with both fighters feeling their way and sounding out their opponent. Tyson came out quickest and landed a couple of decent jabs while Lewis made his power felt with a couple of uppercuts.

The second round was Lewis's all the way from the bell. After being cautioned by referee Eddie Cotton

for holding and hitting, Lewis landed a beautiful right uppercut and began concentrating on his jab. After being hit by a second uppercut, Tyson – realising that he was having difficulty getting to the champion – began lunging in the vain hope that one of his punches would land somewhere near the mark. This strategy didn't work, however, as Lewis continued landing telling punches. By the end of the round, Lewis was in complete control and a dazed Tyson wasn't sure what to do next.

Although Tyson did come out with a purpose in the third round, it was Lewis who again controlled proceedings with another right hand to the jaw and several accurate jabs. Tyson did manage to land a couple of weak punches but soon found he had been cut over the right eye. This spurred him on and he landed a left hook on Lewis's head before the champion scored well with a combination.

The fourth round saw a continuation of the one-sided affair, with Lewis consistently getting through with his punches while Tyson seemed to be unable to stop or evade them. A fierce right from Lewis saw the cut over Tyson's eye worsen but more alarming was the sight of "Iron" Mike walking into punches he used to dodge with ease. Several more vicious punches followed before Lewis was docked a point for pushing Tyson to the canvas.

His corner worked hard between rounds to patch up his right eye, but was left with twice as much work after the fifth round. Lewis inflicted even more damage on his face with several pinpoint jabs and rights that

Lennox Lewis lands a solid right jab on Mike Tyson (L) during round seven of their WBC/IBF/IBO World Heavyweight Championship bout at the Pyramid Arena in Memphis, Tennessee, 8th June 2002. Lewis defeated Tyson by a knockout in the eighth round to retain his championship titles

Lennox Lewis and Mike Tyson in the second round

split the skin over Tyson's left eye. The demolition was almost complete and small pools of blood were beginning to spatter the canvas.

Now having difficulty seeing, Tyson suffered even more punishment in the sixth round. Lewis, with the outcome firmly in his hands, took the fight and systematically concentrated on making his shots count. He landed fierce rights, lefts and uppercuts that left Tyson trudging to his corner at the sound of the bell.

While Tyson came out at the start of the seventh, it wasn't long before normal service was resumed and he again found himself on the receiving end of Lewis's battering rams. A series of jabs and punches left Tyson's nose bleeding in sympathy with his eyes and it was clear that the fight was not going to last much longer.

In fact, it didn't even last one more round as a calculating Lewis bade his time while landing accurate punches. A trio of uppercuts saw Tyson's knees give way but he didn't actually go down. The referee gave him a mandatory eight count nonetheless and Lewis followed this up with another crashing right hand to the jaw which this time did send the American to the canvas. With blood pouring down his face, Tyson clutched his glove to his right eye and was counted out.

Lewis, who relinquished his IBF title, went on to successfully defend against Vitali Klitschko the following year when the fight was stopped due to a cut suffered by the Ukrainian before retiring. Tyson, however, found his indestructible tag was a thing of the past and – although he beat Clifford Etienne – lost twice in succession to Danny Williams and Kevin McBride.

Lennox Lewis stands over Mike Tyson as Tyson hits the mat after a knock-out in the eighth round

Europe's Paul McGinley celebrates after winning the Ryder Cup for Europe on the last day of the 34th Ryder Cup at the Belfry near Birmingham 29th September 2002. McGinley beat Jim Furyk of the U.S in their singles match.

A scene showing Montgomerie and Harrington at the Ryder Cup, 2002

Paul McGinley celebrates his nationality at the 2002 Ryder Cup

2002
RYDER CUP:
EUROPE WIN

The 34th Ryder Cup was scheduled for the Belfry once again and the two teams – from the US and Europe – were as ever both anxious for victory. The 24 players that made up the teams gave their all and each match was a fierce competition that ended in victory for the European team. Sam Torrance's team had claimed a 15½-12½ triumph that culminated in a huge party for both teams at the end of the third day.

The Irishman Paul McGinley was instrumental in the final outcome when he putted 11 feet for the hole on the 18th green. Like many before him he was the hero of the hour including Christy O'Connor Jr in 1989 at the Belfry, Philip Walton in 1995 at Oak Hill and Costantino Rocca in 1997 at Valderrama. The Belfry had also been the setting when in 1985 Sam Torrance himself had been the one to putt the ball at the 18th for a deciding win over the US. The final day was full of tension and the singles matches were dramatic. The three-point lead was also the European team's biggest marginal win over the US since Sam Torrance's performance nearly 20 years earlier.

At the start of the final day, the scores were level at eight each. Torrance decided to send in the "big guns" first in order to gain points and step up momentum. The formula proved to be a good strategy as Colin Montgomerie won by one stroke over his American counterpart Scott Hoch. Bernhard Langer won his match against Hal Sutton while Padraig Harrington added a further point when he defeated Mark Calcavecchia. Darren Clarke also won his match against David Duval although Sergio Garcia conceded to David Toms by one stroke. Scott Verplank then triumphed over Lee Westwood and the European team were only two points ahead.

The excitement mounted as Niclas Fasth, who matched Paul Azinger's game across all 18 greens, stepped onto the course for Europe. However the experienced American managed to gain an extra half point at the end of the match. Phillip Price was decidedly a hero when he won over Phil Mickelson. Swede Pierre Fulke gained a half point against Davis Love III and Jesper Parnevik – also from Sweden – managed another half when Tiger Woods conceded a four-foot par putt on the 18th green. All was left to play for and the pressure fell on rookie McGinley to perform. For most of his match against Jim Furyk, McGinley was trailing behind the American giant – he needed just a half point to win for Europe. He putted a birdie four at the 17th to level the scores and with his sensational 11-foot putt he ensured that the Ryder Cup would be travelling east across the North Atlantic Ocean.

It seems that as captain Torrance was inspirational. He had conversed with Manchester United manager Sir Alex Ferguson and the former golfing star readily acknowledges that he learnt a great deal from Fergie. One of the most important tips that Sir Alex passed on was that there are no major players, no superstars in a team. Everyone is just as crucial as the next person

and that's the way Torrance decided to play it. Part of Torrance's preparations included speaking to players individually a number of times and often at great lengths. He spoke to all the players on the putting green before the match began and he also walked all 12 players to the first tee.

Colin Montgomerie was also a leading factor in the European side's inspirational edge. He remained calm and relaxed and provided a backbone that held the team together and focused. Sam Torrance was particularly impressed with Monty's approach. Bernhard Langer was also another foundation for the team to build on and showed his abilities as a leader when he suggested that Paul McGinley take the first shot when Darren Clarke found himself in a bunker. The excellent shot from McGinley put the pressure on the US partnership of Scott Hoch and Jim Furyk. Colin Montgomerie also obtained four and a half points out of five and earned himself much praise for the steadfast lead he gave the rest of the team.

Despite defeat, US captain Curtis Strange remained upbeat remarking that although it was disappointing to lose the match it certainly didn't spoil the event and he readily agreed that the European team had played better golf than the US side.

The outstanding players of the match were undoubtedly Montgomerie who was only the third man (following the two Spaniards, Ballesteros and Olazabal) to gain a score of four and a half while David Toms was the best American rookie (along with Chip Beck) with a final score of three and a half points. Both Thomas Bjorn and Padraig Harrington remained undefeated in Ryder Cup singles while Jim Furyk remained unbeaten in his three singles games with two and a half points out of three. Phillip Price gave Phil Mickelson his first singles defeat and Bernhard Langer repeated his 1985 success in the singles over Hal Sutton.

2003 RUGBY WORLD CUP: ENGLAND V AUSTRALIA

Aspirations were high as England started their 2003 World Cup campaign, having won three of the last four Six Nations championships with the most recent seeing them record their 12th Grand Slam title. They went into the tournament as joint favourites with New Zealand, although South Africa and Australia were expected to be strong contenders as usual.

Originally intended to be co-hosted by Australia and New Zealand, the tournament was staged purely in Australia after a dispute over ground signage rights. After a change in qualification for the 1999 World Cup, this time round saw a return to the eight quarter-finalists from the previous tournament gaining automatic entry. The remaining 12 places were fought over by a record 81 nations.

Both Australia and England came through the group stage with a 100% record. The Wallabies cruised to victories over Argentina (24-8), Romania (90-8) and Namibia (142-0) before emerging victorious from a close-fought encounter with Ireland (17-16). England, meanwhile, qualified with wins over Georgia (84-6), South Africa (25-6), Samoa (35-22) and Uruguay (111-13) to set up a quarter-final clash with Wales.

The Welsh put up a good fight and scored three tries – Stephen Jones, Colin Charvis and Martyn Williams – but it was the boot of Jonny Wilkinson that did the damage, scoring six penalties, a drop goal and converting Will Greenwood's try. Australia found themselves paired with Scotland but eased into the semi-finals with tries from Stirling Mortlock, George Gregan and David Lyons giving them a 33-16 triumph.

The semi-finals saw two northern hemisphere teams and two southern hemisphere sides pitched against each other as Australia faced the All Blacks while England took on France. The Wallabies had the boot of Elton Flatley to thank for their 22-10 win while England relied totally on Wilkinson's kicking to secure their 24-7 victory with five penalties and three drop goals. This set up a repeat of the 1991 final, that Australia had won 12-6.

The final itself took place in Sydney's Telstra Stadium on 22nd November 2003 and Australia put the first points on the scoreboard when winger Lote Tuqiri outjumped Jason Robinson to catch a Stephen Larkham up and under after just six minutes. Fly-half Jonny Wilkinson soon had England in front with two penalties before the Whites were presented with a try-scoring opportunity. Unfortunately, Ben Kay failed to collect the ball from Matt Dawson's pass and knocked on when it seemed easier to score.

Following a third Wilkinson penalty, England moved further in front when Lawrence Dallaglio made ground before passing to Wilkinson who found Robinson steaming up on his left shoulder. The pass was timed to perfection and Robinson registered the second try of the game to send England in with a half-time lead of 14-5.

The second half, however, saw the Australians put nine points on the board with England failing to add to their tally. As can so often be their undoing, England gave away two needless penalties which allowed Elton Flatley to close the gap to three points. Then, with 90 seconds of normal time left on the clock, England were

Jonny Wilkinson raises his arms after England beat Australia

Jonny Wilkinson kicks a drop goal to win the Rugby World Cup

penalised for collapsing a scrum and Flatley levelled the match to send the game into extra-time.

After Wilkinson had again put England in front with another penalty, Australia were awarded a penalty of their own after England held on to the ball on the floor with two minutes to go and Flatley equalised at 17-17. Then came the moment that every England fan will remember for the rest of their lives and that every Australian cannot wait to forget.

With just over one minute remaining on the clock, England won a line-out and drove towards the Australian line. Everybody in the stadium knew that they were waiting to give Wilkinson the opportunity to kick for goal. The fly-half, the youngest member of the squad, had already missed two drop goal attempts but still had enough confidence to try again.

Three times England tried to drive through the Australian defence before Dawson decided to pass back to Wilkinson who was sitting in the pocket. The England number 10 kept a cool head and gave a

perfect demonstration of how to kick a drop goal. The ball flew through the posts with just 28 seconds left on the clock and England had won the World Cup before the match went to a sudden-death decision.

Martin Johnson lifted the William Webb Ellis trophy but England suffered a torrid time over the next few years, finishing third and fourth in the following two Six Nations championships and embarking on a seven-match losing streak in 2006. Wilkinson himself suffered a series of injuries and didn't play for his country after the World Cup final until February 2007 when he inspired England to victory in the Calcutta Cup match against Scotland.

Matt Dawson (L) and Ben Cohen celebrate their win

Prince Harry (R) poses with England coach Clive Woodward

Annika Sorenstam celebrates a birdie on the 13th green during the first round of the Bank of America Colonial

2003 ANNIKA SORENSTAM CONTENDS PGA

As for many years, since her professional career began back in 1993, Annika Sorenstam (born on 9th October 1970 in Sweden) ended 2002 as the indisputable top women's golfer of the year. Her earnings were reported to be nearly £3 million and she set a new record scoring average of 68.7 securing herself an induction into the LPGA Hall of Fame. But 2003 was to prove a testing year for Sorenstam when she made her debut on the PGA tour.

The year began with five LPGA events during the opening months where she registered five top 10 finishes including her win at the Office Depot Championship. However Sorenstam then announced that she was to play in the Fort Worth at Hogan's Alley having been invited to participate by the organisers of the Colonial. There were mixed feelings about Sorenstam's involvement, from Vijay Singh's outspoken concern that a woman was being allowed to take part in a man's competition, to those who supported the world's leading lady. Despite trying to ignore and avoid the rising controversy, Sorenstam herself admitted that rather than wanting to make a stand for women's golf she was merely wanting to test the limits of her own game. Had Sorenstam been a man her achievements would probably have hit the headlines and praise for the leading golfer would have been high. Spurred on by the mediocre attention she received Sorenstam was probably keen to prove her worth at the next level in sporting achievement.

Sorenstam was widely supported by the crowd that attended on day one when she walked towards the first tee, even if some fellow competitors were not. Her playing partners were also in full support as both Aaron Barber and Dean Wilson declared themselves honoured to be a part of history in the making. Both men helped to calm the nervous woman player and Sorenstam soon settled into a comfortable game. Her first round was fairly typical of her excellent previous performances but the pressure of playing in front of huge crowds was clearly visible by the second round. It was as though the world's number one was trying to please the crowds and hampered by nerves never really found herself in her stride. Indeed Sorenstam almost had to catch up to make par. She ended up with a succession of bogeys leading to a score of 74. Despite being the end of Sorenstam's stab at the tournament she received the largest standing ovation of the event. The world's leading woman golfer was overwhelmed – unusually – by emotion and stated later that although the experience had been exhilarating she would not be contesting the Colonial in the future. The shame was that too many critics – including fellow competitors – uttered a collective huge sigh of relief.

Annika Sorenstam began playing golf at the age of 12 supported by her parents and her sister Lotta Sorenstam (also a professional golfer). In 1995 she won the Athlete of the Year Award – Sweden's most prestigious sports award. She enjoyed a successful amateur career and was a member of the Swedish national team between 1987 and 1992. Sorenstam became the World Amateur Champion in 1992 and came in at second place in the US Women's Amateur Championship.

Annika Sorenstam at the PGA

In her first year as a professional in 1993, Sorenstam found herself Rookie of the Year on the European Tour. Her major tournaments include the 1995 US Women's Open, the 1996 US Women's Open, the 1997 Chrysler-Plymouth Tournament of Champions, the Michelob Light Classic in 1998 and then again in 1999. Sorenstam also won the 2000 Welch's/Circle K Championship which she won again the following year along with the Nabisco Championship and the 2002 LPGA Takefuji Classic. This prolific player has also competed in the Solheim Cup representing Europe in 1994, 1996, 1998, 2000, 2002, 2003 and 2005. On 9 August 2002 Sorenstam missed the cut at the Women's British Open at Turnberry which was her first missed cut in 74 tournaments since she missed the US Open in 1999.

Sorenstam is one of the most successful women golfers in the world. She has won 69 official LPGA tournaments, including 10 major tournaments. Between 2000 and 2005, she won at least five tournaments each year and she tops the LPGA's career money list by several million dollars and is estimated to have earnings of more than $20 million. Sorenstam is also the holder of a number of scoring records including the lowest score in a single round which she achieved at the 2001 Standard Register PING tournament with a staggering score of 59. She has won the Vare Trophy six times which is given to the player with the lowest scoring average in a season.

During her educational years, Sorenstam moved to the US where she played collegiate golf for the University of Arizona. Sorenstam had an exceptional year and added more impressive wins to her already impressive record. She defended her title in the MasterCard Classic in 2006 and won the US Women's Open along with the Women's World Cup of Golf for Sweden with partner Liselotte Neumann.

Annika Sorenstam celebrates after winning the 12th hole during the morning foursomes of the 2003 Solheim Cup

Brian Lara hits out during the second day of the second cricket test against England at Edgbaston in Birmingham, 30th July 2004

2004
WEST INDIES V ENGLAND, ANTIGUA: LARA REGAINS RECORD

In 1994, Brian Lara set a new record for the highest individual innings in Test cricket. Against a hapless England attack on the Recreation Ground in St John's, Antigua, he played a major role in the West Indies' 3-1 series win. Amid scenes of great jubilation, he scored 375 to pass the previous record of 365 not out, set by Garry Sobers in Kingston, Jamaica, in 1958 against Pakistan. Present at the ground when Lara assumed his mantle, Sir Garfield went out to the middle to congratulate him in person.

He might not have noticed that in pulling the record-breaking runs, Lara had dislodged a bail that fortuitously fell back into the groove. It was just about the only piece of good fortune he needed in an otherwise flawless innings. That was not the case when Lara set a new first-class record just a couple of months later. Playing for

Warwickshire against Durham at Edgbaston, he scored 501 not out in a match that was destined to be a draw after a day's play was lost to rain. The good luck Lara enjoyed in that innings came when he was on just 18. He was dropped by Durham wicket-keeper Chris Scott, who turned to first slip and said forlornly, "I bet he goes on to get a hundred now."

Lara lost the Test record when Matthew Hayden scored 380 for Australia against a very ordinary Zimbabwe side in Perth in October 2003. But Hayden was to hold it for only six months before Lara snatched it back again, in rather different circumstances to those of a decade earlier. Antigua was again the setting and England were again the opponents, but they were a much stronger side, while Lara was captain of the humbled West Indies.

England had won the first three Tests, and were on the

England players mob Andrew Flintoff after West Indies Captain Brian Lara was caught out during play on the first day of the third test

Brian Lara hits out during the second day of the second cricket test against England

verge of a whitewash to avenge the two "blackwashes" inflicted upon them by the West Indies in the 1980s. Lara was under particular pressure as so much was expected of him, yet thus far he had failed to deliver. His scores were 23 and nought in Jamaica, nought and eight in Trinidad, followed by 36 and 33 in Barbados. Exactly 100 runs at an average of 16.66 was not what his Caribbean public expected.

He did the first thing right by winning the toss on the usual St John's batting paradise. In another manifestation of the changing order, England's pace attack had been irresistible earlier in the series, but they found the surface at the Recreation Ground to be anything but good for their health. They managed to dismiss Darren Ganga for 10 when the score was 33 in the 14th over, but that brought Lara to the crease early.

As memories of 10 years earlier came flooding back, so too did his form. The outfield was as fast as the pitch was true, enabling Chris Gayle to reach a fifty that included 10 boundaries, before he was out to the last ball before lunch. Rain then prevented any play until after four o'clock, but there was still time for Lara to put on a hundred with Ramnaresh Sarwan before stumps. Lara was undefeated on 81 out of 208 for two.

England's whitewash aspirations gave way to perspiration on the second day.

Their attack toiled through 105 overs, after which the West Indies were in total command on 595 for five. Sarwan had put on 232 with Lara, but once he had gone for 90, Ricardo Powell and Ryan Hinds followed relatively cheaply. Ridley Jacobs then joined Lara to provide ideal support for his fellow left-hander.

Lara was 313 not out overnight, and although some critics accused him of selfishness when he batted on, after three consecutive defeats he wanted to make the game safe before entertaining any idea of winning it. He reached lunch with the total on 734 for five. Jacobs had his hundred, and Lara himself had gone past Hayden's 380 to dine with 390 to his name. Few now begrudged him what might have been thought of as an indulgence, in reappearing after the interval to reach 400. In all, it took him 773 minutes; he faced 582 balls and hit 43 fours and four sixes.

A deflated England made only 285 in their first innings but, following on, reached 422 for five for the match to finish in stalemate. The West Indies had their face-saving draw, while the record was back in the Caribbean, in Lara's possession once again. Of all the great names that grace that particular list of batsmen, only one appears twice: Brian Charles Lara.

*Liverpool captain Steven Gerrard lifts the European Cup after Liverpool wins the European Champions League final on
25th May 2005 at the Ataturk Olympic Stadium in Istanbul, Turkey*

2005 CHAMPIONS LEAGUE: LIVERPOOL V AC MILAN

Liverpool achieved a staggering victory over AC Milan in 2005, culminating in a penalty shoot-out to win the Champions League after amazingly coming from three goals down at half-time. On a night that has become known to fans as the "miracle of Istanbul", Liverpool reclaimed their crown as "kings of Europe" after overcoming a seemingly insurmountable challenge at the Ataturk Stadium in Istanbul.

The 2005 UEFA Champions League Final was the final match of the 2004–05 UEFA Champions League. The showpiece event took place on 25st May 2005. Liverpool, who had won the competition four times, were appearing in their sixth final, and their first since 1985. Milan, who had won the competition six times, were appearing in their second final in three years and tenth overall. It was the Reds' first appearance in a European Cup final in two decades and, despite defeating Juventus and Chelsea during a memorable run to the final, they went into the game as underdogs. Milan were seen by all as the favourites. Their team included many experienced players who had played in the competition previously. Liverpool's manager was Rafael Benítez. He acknowledged the perceived imbalance. "Maybe Milan are favourites, but we have confidence, and we can win," he said.

An estimated 40,000 fans followed their team to Istanbul. But, by the time the half-time whistle came, it was looking as though their trip was in vain. Paolo Maldini gave AC Milan a lead within the first minute of the match. Hernan Crespo then went on to score a double. All of which appeared to give the team an unassailable advantage. Milan added a third goal when Kaka brilliantly passed to Crespo. Then came half-time.

After some serious half-time discussions between players and manager, Liverpool managed to reinvigorate themselves. Rallying cries from still-believing supporters helped, too, providing just the added impetus to hopefully tip the balance.

Liverpool substituted Dietmar Hamann in place of Steve Finnan. They also changed to a 3–5–2 formation, with Riise and Šmicer on the outside edges, Alonso and Hamann as holding midfielders and Gerrard as an attacking midfielder.

Liverpool seized the advantage early on with Xabi Alonso sending the ball narrowly past Milan's right hand post. Dudek managed a save against Shevchenko's free-kick to stop Liverpool going four down. Steven Gerrard managed to provide some cheer for Liverpool, while Vladimir Smicer and Xabi Alonso fought back and brought things to a symmetrical balance, equalizing.

Gerrard offered Liverpool further promise of salvation with a header from John Arne Riise's cross. This also helped to bring some life back to the team; and now the fight-back was in earnest. This was evidenced when Gennaro Gattuso pulled out all the stops to bring down Gerrard just as he was about to equalize. Dida saw off Alonso's attack, but the Spanish midfielder returned to produce the goods. Milan could only look on as their victory looked to be falling apart.

In extra time, Milan launched a fight-back. They managed to keep possession for most of the remaining half-hour and nearly scored in the final minutes. Then came the penalty shoot-outs.

Serginho and Pirlo missed Milan's first two, while Hamann and Djibril Cisse hit the button for Liverpool. Andriy Shevchenko was the third Milan player to miss a penalty, making it look like the end was both near and inevitable. Jerzy Dudek managed to see off goal attempts from Andrea Pirlo and Andriy Shevchenko in the nail-biting finish to clinch a stunning victory for Liverpool.

The city of Liverpool celebrated their victory by parading the trophy around town in an open-top double-decker bus the day after the final. They were cheered by around a million supporters. Benítez expressed his own disbelief at the stunning victory. "My problem is that I don't have words to express the things that I feel at this moment," he said.

Diego Maradona was also impressed. "Even the Brazil team that won the 1970 World Cup could not have staged a comeback with Milan leading 3–0...The English club proved that miracles really do exist," he said. "I've now made Liverpool my English team. They showed that football is the most beautiful sport of all. You knew they could defend, but the team showed they could play too and wrote a page in the history books. The match will last forever. The Liverpool supporters didn't let me go to sleep the night before. There were 10 of them to every three Milan supporters. They showed their unconditional support at half-time when they were losing 3–0 and still they didn't stop singing."

The victory marked an amazing turnaround for Liverpool, who had looked as thought they had little chance in the first half of the match. They had already upset the status quo with their very appearance in

the final. This was Liverpool's fifth European Cup. The win in Istanbul meant they qualified for the 2005 FIFA Club World Championship. In this, Liverpool beat Deportivo Saprissa 3–0 in the semi-final, and played Copa Libertadores champions São Paulo in the final, losing 1–0.

Following the Istanbul win, they were awarded the trophy permanently, and claimed a multiple-winner badge. The "miracle of Istanbul" is now regarded as one of the greatest finals in the history of the tournament – and one of the most astounding comebacks in the history of sport.

Liverpool celebrate after they win European Champions League final

Liverpool's goalkeeper Jerzy Dudek celebrates with a TV camera after winning

Liverpool captain Steven Gerrard lifts the European Cup

AC Milan's Brazilian forward Kaka (L) hugs AC Milan's Italian captain and defender Paolo Maldini (C) after he scored an opening goal

Lewis Hamilton celebrates his win at the United States Grand Prix in Indianapolis, Indiana

2007
THE HAMILTON EFFECT

From the moment the 2007 Formula One season commenced at Australia's Albert Park circuit in Melbourne, it was clear, even to those who display nothing more than a casual interest in the sport, that there was a true star in the ascendancy.

At just 22 years old, British driver Lewis Hamilton had taken motor racing's premier class by storm and embarrassed many seasoned campaigners in the process with a level of maturity that belies his years and an incredible grasp of race-craft that echoes the likes of Senna, Stewart and Schumacher. It is, therefore, no coincidence that Jackie Stewart himself has tipped the youngster to take the World Drivers'

Championship title in his debut year or that Michael Schumacher has expressed surprise at his ability to consistently deliver results.

Hamilton was born in Stevenage, Hertfordshire, in January 1985 and experienced his first taste of motor sport racing his radio-controlled car at the age of five. Within a year, he was so proficient at its controls that he appeared on BBC television's Blue Peter. Nobody could have guessed where that first interest in four-wheeled sport would take him. That year, his father bought him his first go-kart and once more he took to it like a duck to water. After a couple of years he started racing and soon began to win on a regular basis.

Opposite: Hamilton celebrates his win as his father Anthony (bottom) applauds, in the Japanese F1 Grand Prix at Fuji Speedway in Oyama, September 30, 2007

At the age of 9, he was introduced to McLaren team principal Ron Dennis at which point he asked if he could race for the team in the future. Four years later, their paths crossed again when Hamilton was signed to the McLaren driver development support programme becoming the youngest ever driver to secure a contract in Formula 1. Hamilton's karting career culminated in 2000 when he won the European Formula A Championship with maximum points and the Formula A World Cup.

Following his karting success a move to cars was inevitable. In 2003, he won the Formula Renault UK Championship for Manor Motorsports scoring an impressive 11 pole positions and 10 wins from 15 starts. In 2004, Hamilton moved to Formula 3 finishing fifth in the Championship before going on to take the title in 2005 at his second attempt. Next followed a move to the fiercely competitive, 21 race GP2 Series. With five wins to his name, he took the title at his first attempt once again bringing his exploits to the attention of Dennis.

To the amazement of the Formula 1 world, he was signed to drive for Vodafone McLaren Mercedes for the 2007 season. This was a significant moment for the driver, the team and the sport as a whole. For Hamilton, he was realising a life's ambition in taking his seat behind the controls of a Formula 1 racing car. For the team it was a big gamble – Hamilton was young and inexperienced and, it was argued, there were others who deserved the seat more. For the sport it was the first time a black driver had been seen in the Formula 1 paddock.

Hamilton did not disappoint. In his first race at Melbourne, he stunned the world by qualifying in fourth place obscuring experienced drivers like Giancarlo Fisichella and Ralf Schumacher. But this achievement was soon eclipsed by his race performance where he finished third behind Ferrari's Kimi Räikkönen and his own team mate, reigning world champion Fernando Alonso.

In doing so, Hamilton became the first driver to finish on the podium in his debut race since Jacques Villeneuve in 1996.

Fantastic as this was, many assumed that this was just a flash in the pan moment for a precociously talented youngster. They were quickly proved wrong when three weeks later he went one better: qualifying in fourth once again but finishing second in the race behind Alonso. His form continued to Bahrain the following week where he qualified on the front row alongside pole-sitter Felipe Massa's Ferrari whilst his team mate was relegated to fourth behind Räikkönen.

At the fourth round of the championship, held on the Catalunya circuit in Spain, Hamilton again qualified in fourth position behind Massa, Alonso and Räikkönen. As the race got away on its second attempt (the first being aborted after Jarno Trulli stalled his Toyota on the grid) Alonso and Massa charged into the first corner but the warring pair touched sending the World Champion into the gravel. All of a sudden Hamilton found himself running in second place whist his team mate battled to make up for lost ground. Despite a fire in the pits almost putting an end to his race, Felipe Massa went on to take the win but Hamilton had valiantly held onto his position to take his third second-placed finish of the season and in doing so had become the youngest ever driver to lead the World Drivers' Championship. Whether, as Frank Williams described him, he truly is superhuman remains to be seen. What is certain is that Lewis Hamilton is set to be one of the greatest Formula 1 drivers of all time.

*Lewis Hamilton celebrates his win at the Canadian F1 Grand Prix in
Montreal, 10th June 2007*

2007
INDIA V PAKISTAN

The first ICC World Twenty20 took place in South Africa in September 2007. 12 teams took part in the thirteen-day tournament and the final was a truly historic moment in cricketing history – an epic battle between two of cricket's greatest teams, India and Pakistan.

India won the toss and chose to bat first. Umar Gul took the wickets of both Yuvraj Singh and Mahendra Singh Dhoni, leaving India with 157 for 5 in 20 overs. But RP Singh hit back twice early on and Irfan Pathan took 3-16 as the Pakistani team began to relinquish their wickets. Misbah-ul-Haq (43) helped his team recover somewhat with three sixes off Harbhajan Singh and another in the final over, but ended up falling to Joginder Sharma.

A 21-run over from Sreesanth gave Pakistan another advantage. But Irfan Pathan (3-16) and Joginder Sharma (2-20) slowed this progress down significantly. With Pakistan needing 54 from 24 balls, Misbah-ul-Haq hit three sixes off Harbhajan Singh in one over. Sreesanth was also out for two sixes but took the wicket of Sohail Tanvir, as Pakistan went into the last over needing 13 runs to win, with only one wicket remaining.

Gautam Gambhir remained calm after newcomer Yusuf Pathan and Robin Uthappa were out during a feverish opening. Perfect placement aided him in attaining a fifty in 38 balls. The left-hander put India on course for an unassailable total, but Yuvraj Singh was unable to get started as Gul took command. India would still

Irfan Pathan of India celebrates the wicket of Yasir Arafat of Pakistan for 15 runs during the Twenty20 Championship Final match

Irfan Pathan and his team mates celebrate the wicket of Shoib Malik of Pakistan for 6 runs

have to find the energy to match the challenge, if they wanted to bag their first big trophy since 1985. If Imran Nazir was able to remain at the crease, India's run rate would likely remain favourable. He managed to pull off two fours and two sixes. Less persuasive was Younus Khan. However, he did help to take the team past 50 in the sixth over.

The game then changed pace, as Dhoni's bowling changes took the pace off the ball. Consequently, the score changed to 52/2 to 77/6. Nazir was off the crease when Uthappa's throw hit the stumps, while India fought back and RP Singh took three wickets. Shoaib Malik and dangerman Shahid Afridi, who had gone first ball, lost their wickets with determined throws from Irfan Pathan. Misbah swayed Harbhajan for three huge sixes, while Tanvir hit Santh for two more maximums.

Then came a crucial moment in the match. Santh demolished the tail-ender's off-stump and RP Singh finished off Gul. The inexperienced Joginder Sharma

was entrusted with the final over and began with a horrible wide and when Misbah battered another six down the ground the game looked up.

Misbah's speculative gambit of trying to hike the ball over short fine-leg backfired and handed the resounding victory to India. The impressive wickets of RP Singh and Irfan Pathan had turned the fortunes of the game around.

"The way Gul and Yasir Arafat bowled was excellent but we knew one thing: if you can get quick wickets and pressurise the batsmen it gets really hard," said Dhoni. "Our bowling was consistent throughout the tournament and one of the main reasons for us winning it.

The victorious team's success earned them a cash bonus of £1.5m from the Indian cricket board, while Yuvraj Singh netted £125,000 for hitting six sixes in an over against England. Irfan Pathan was awarded the Man of the Match award.

2008 BEIJING OLYMPICS: USAIN BOLT

To date, Usain Bolt boasts nine of the 30 fastest 100 metre times in history, as well as holding the 200 m world record. He continues to be celebrated alongside the world's greatest sporting heroes including Muhammad Ali, Michael Phelps and Sir Donald Bradman. Yet despite this impressive status, Bolt's rise to stardom was not typical by any means. Unlike most athletes, Bolt didn't have a clear path from the start. His abilities varied from track to pitch, as he competed at high jump events, while also proving himself to be a talented fast bowler in cricket.

In 2001, Bolt narrowed his focus and he began to channel his energy on the track. He competed at the reputable CARIFTA Trials (an annual athletics competition in the Caribbean), and won the 200 m and 400m doubles; finally, people started taking notice of the young, sporting prodigy. That same year, Bolt won four gold medals at the meet in Nassau, Bahamas. Since these events, his rise in popularity was meteoric. In 2007, he broke the Jamaican 200m record with a time of 19.75 seconds.

However, it was during the Olympic games in Beijing, in the summer of 2008, that Bolt truly made his mark and demonstrated his extraordinary sprinting abilities. Prior to Beijing, Bolt announced that he would double-up and compete in both the 100 m and 200 m events. As a 100 m world-record holder, Bolt was a firm favourite to win both events. His talent was supported by sprinting legend, Michael Johnson, who dismissed critics' claims that Bolt's lack of experience would hinder his chances of victory.

This doubt was soon quashed. It was during the 100 m final that Bolt broke the record as he reached the finishing line in 9.69 seconds (unofficially 9.683 seconds) with an extraordinary reaction time of 0.165 seconds. This time beat his personal best and Bolt was well ahead of second-place finisher, Richard Thompson (finishing time: 9.89 seconds), making the win all the more impressive. Following this, the athlete won Jamaica's fourth gold medal (during Beijing), establishing a new world and Olympic record of 19.30 seconds. He beat previous winner Michael Johnson's record of 19.32 seconds. Bolt became the first sprinter to break both records simultaneously at the same Olympic games. Two days later, Bolt competed as the third leg in the Jamaican 4 x 100 m relay team, alongside teammates Nesta Carter, Asafa Powell and Michael Frater. Together, they broke another world and Olympic record, finishing in 37.10 seconds*.

The world watched in awe as Bolt secured a triple-win in the 100 m, 200 m and 4 x 100 m, all in world record times. He rewrote the history books and achieved one of the biggest sports performances of all time.

Following the Beijing triple victory, Bolt continued to impress the sporting world as he took three gold medals in the same events during the 2012 Olympic Games in London. This event gave him undivided global attention as his record-breaking performance made him the world's fastest man. His performance went from strength-to-strength as he continued to win titles in Rio (2016), as well as the IAAF World T&F Championships in Berlin, Daegu, Moscow & Beijing.

plant
parts

Flowers

Melanie Waldron

Raintree

Raintree is an imprint of Capstone Global Library Limited, a company incorporated in England and Wales having its registered office at 7 Pilgrim Street, London, EC4V 6LB – Registered company number: 6695582

www.raintreepublishers.co.uk
myorders@raintreepublishers.co.uk

Text © Capstone Global Library Limited 2014
First published in hardback in 2014
The moral rights of the proprietor have been asserted.

Edited by Sian Smith and Adrian Vigliano
Designed by Cynthia Akiyoshi
Original illustrations © HL Studios
Illustrated by HL Studios
Picture research by Mica Brancic
Originated by Capstone Global Library Ltd
Printed in China by CTPS

ISBN 978 1 406 27477 6
17 16 15 14 13
10 9 8 7 6 5 4 3 2 1

British Library Cataloguing in Publication Data
Waldron, Melanie
Flowers (Plant parts)
A full catalogue record for this book is available from the British Library.

Acknowledgements
We would like to thank the following for permission to reproduce photographs: Alamy p. 10 (© Emilio Ereza); Capstone Publishers pp. 10, 11, 14, 15 (© Karon Dubke); Naturepl. com pp. 4 (© Ernie Janes), 17 (© Robert Thompson), 19 (© Paul Harcourt Davies), 21 (© Rolf Nussbaumer), 22 (© Nature Production), 23 (© Adrian Davies), 26 (© Laurie Campbell), 27 (© Jabruson), 29 (2020VISION/© Paul Harris), 20 main (© Visuals Unlimited), 25 main (© Tim Laman); Press Association p. 24 main (Scanpix Norway/Trond J Strom); Science Photo Library p. 7 (Maryann Frazier); Shutterstock pp. 5 (© trucic), 8 (© wjarek), 9 (© Marykit), 13 (© tr3gin), 17 (© BMJ), 18 (© Mr. Green), 28 (© Polina Shestakova), 16 top (© V.Borisov), 20 inset (© vnlit), 24 inset (© bergamont), 25 inset (© Marcel Mooij), imprint page (© nbriam), title page (© Iryna Rasko).

Cover photograph reproduced with permission of Shutterstock (© Iryna Rasko).

We would like to thank Michael Bright for his invaluable help in the preparation of this book.

Contents

Some words are shown in bold, **like this**. You can find out what they mean by looking in the glossary.

Flowers all around us

Look outside! You will see that most gardens, parks, and meadows all have flowers growing in them. There are many different colours, shapes, and sizes of flowers.

Some flowers are very large and colourful. Others are much smaller and duller. You may not even notice some flowers. Most trees have very small flowers, and even grasses have flowers. In fact, most plants make flowers. Flowering plants are the biggest group of plants.

There are lots of different types of flowers. Although they may look different, they have lots of things in common.

Not all flowers grow in fields and meadows. This flower is growing on a cactus in the desert.

What are flowers for?

Plants have flowers so they can make seeds. Seeds can then grow into new plants. Different plants have different ways of making sure their flowers make seeds. Plants that don't have flowers have different ways of making new plants.

Ancient plants

There have been flowering plants on Earth for around 145 million years! The flowering plants that were around that long ago are different from the ones we see today. However, they did the same job as today's flowers – making seeds.

Parts of a plant

As well as flowers, plants have lots of different parts. **Roots** are the plant parts that grow underground. They hold the plant in the ground. They also take in water and **nutrients** that the plant needs to grow. The plant's **stem** rises from the ground. It holds the plant upright and it contains tiny tubes. Water, nutrients, and food travel through these tubes.

flower

This diagram shows the parts of flowering plants.

leaf

stem

roots

This plant is bending towards the light, because its leaves need light to make food.

Food factories

Plant leaves have a very special job. They contain a green chemical called **chlorophyll**. This captures sunlight, and turns it into food for the plant. This is called **photosynthesis**. To carry out photosynthesis, the leaves also need water, and a gas from the air called **carbon dioxide**.

The food made in the leaves gives the plant energy to grow, and to make flowers and seeds. Because plants produce food for themselves, they are called **producers**.

Day and night

Plants can only make food for themselves during the day, when there is light. At night, plants move the food they have made around their different parts, to where it is needed most.

Blooming into flower

Most plants don't have flowers all year round. They grow and die at different times in each plant's **life cycle**.

Flowers grow from tiny **buds** on plant stems. Inside these buds, the tiny flower petals are all curled up. **Sepals** surround the outsides of the buds. These protect the petals. As the buds grow, the sepals separate and the flowers start to open out.

sepal

You can see green sepals on this peony flower bud. They have opened up to let the petals open out.

This hogweed plant has flowers shaped like an umbrella at the top of the stem. Plants like these are called umbellifers.

Types of flowers

There are many different shapes and arrangements of flowers. Some are shaped like crosses or stars, for example wood anemones. Some flowers, such as harebells, are shaped like bells or trumpets.

Some plants, such as tulips, have only one flower on each stem. Some have lots of flowers on each stem, for example larkspur. Others, such as meadowsweet, have clusters of tiny flowers.

One single flower?

You might think that a daisy or a sunflower is one single flower. However, the centre part of each one is actually made up of many tiny flowers. These are surrounded by different flowers, each making one petal around the edge.

Try this!

Try this simple activity to see how flowers are different.

You will need:
- a selection of flowers
- a magnifying glass

1 Go with an adult to a flower shop to buy some flowers. Try to pick out as many flowers as you can that look different from each other.

2 Spread all your flowers out on a table and start looking closely at them. Do they have one flower on each stem, or many? Do they have clusters of tiny flowers? Separate them out into groups if you can.

10

3 Now look at the individual flowers on each stem. How many petals are there on each flower? What kind of shape do the petals make?

4 Now think about the overall shape of the flower. Is it round and flattish? It might be trumpet-shaped, like some daffodils, or star-shaped, like some lilies. It might be a very difficult shape to describe!

5 While you are looking at the flowers, can you see the sepals? They are usually green, and lie at the top of the stem before the petals. What other parts of the flowers can you see?

Find out

Why do you think that there are so many different shapes, sizes, and colours of flowers?

Parts of a flower

Different types of flowers can look very different from each other. However, they are all made up of similar parts, each doing a special job.

This diagram shows the different parts of a flower. They all help the plant to make seeds.

anther

carpel

ovary

pollen

stigma

stamen

Sepals – these protect the bud until the flower is ready to open.

stem

Petals – these open up to reveal the parts inside the flower. Some plants have petals that close at night or in cold weather, to protect the delicate parts.

Stalk – this grows from the stem of the plant.

A lily

pollen

stigma

stamen

Male and female parts

Flowers have male and female parts inside them. These work together to make seeds.

Stamen – this is the male part of the flower. The **anther** is at the tip of the stamen. This is where the **pollen** is.

Carpel – this is the female part of the flower. The **stigma** is at the tip of the carpel. The **ovary** is at the bottom of the carpel.

Expensive stamens

Saffron is a spice used in cooking. It is made from dried crocus stamens. It turns the food a bright gold colour. Saffron is very expensive!

13

Try this!

In this activity, you can try to find the different parts of a flower.

You will need:
- a large, simple flower
- scissors
- a magnifying glass

1 Choose a large, simple flower such as a lily or a tulip. Its parts should be large enough for you to see and identify.

2 Very gently and carefully, start to take the flower apart. First, use scissors to cut off the stalk just below the bottom of the flower.

2

3 If you can see sepals on your flower, carefully pull these off.

14

4 One by one, remove the petals from the flower. They should come off quite easily. Count them as you go, to see how many petals there are.

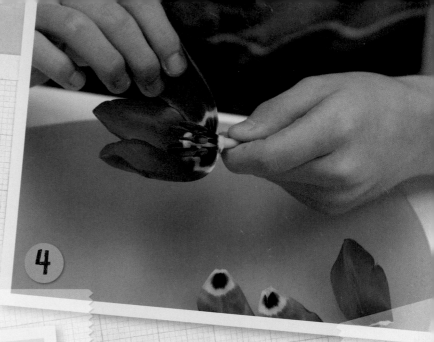

4

5 Once the petals have been removed, only the inside parts of the flower will be left. Look at these closely. Can you see the stamens? Can you see the anther, with pollen on it? Be careful with the pollen – it can stain your clothes! Cut off the stamens with some scissors.

6 Now, all that should be left on your flower is the carpel. This is the female part of the flower.

What next?

Try this again with some different flowers. How are they similar? How are they different?

15

Making seeds

The role of a flower is to make seeds, to grow into new plants. The flower needs pollen and **ovules** to make seeds. Pollen is the male part needed for this. It is found on the anthers. Ovules are the female parts, and they are found inside the plant's ovary.

For a flower to make seeds, pollen from the anthers needs to land on the female part of the flower, called the stigma. This is known as **pollination**. Cells from the pollen then travel down a tube into the ovary, and join up with ovules. This is called **fertilization**. Now the ovules can grow into seeds.

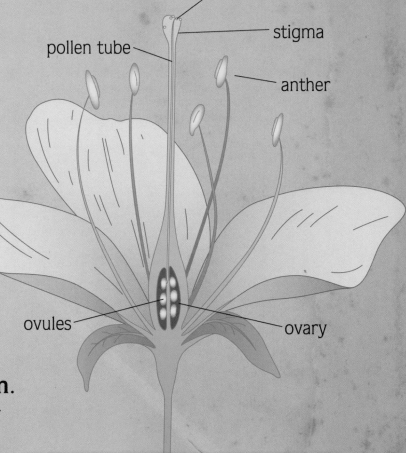

pollen

stigma

pollen tube

anther

ovules

ovary

This diagram shows how pollen can pollinate and fertilize the female part of a flower.

The bee orchid flower can self-pollinate. Its stamens bend over so that the pollen on the anthers can touch the stigma.

Self-pollination

Some flowers can pollinate themselves. This is called **self-pollination**. Seeds produced by self-pollination will grow into plants that are exact copies of the parent plant.

Protecting pollen

Some plants have developed flowers that protect pollen from rain. Bluebells and snowdrops have umbrella-shaped flowers that droop, so rain can't get inside them. Daisies close up their petals at night, protecting the pollen from low temperatures.

17

Attractive flowers

Most flowers are pollinated by pollen from other plants, rather than from their own anthers. This is called **cross-pollination**. Seeds made by cross-pollination grow into plants that are a mix of the two different parent plants.

This moth is drinking nectar from the flower. As it does so, pollen sticks to its long feeding tube.

For cross-pollination to happen, flowers need help to move the pollen between flowers. Lots of different animals provide that help, and flowers have different ways of attracting animals to them. Many produce a sweet, sugary liquid called **nectar**, which animals eat.

Sending signals

Many flowers have special ways of attracting animals. Some have oils in their petals, sepals, pollen, and nectar that give off strong scents. Some have brightly coloured petals that attract different animals. For example, bees like yellow and blue flowers and butterflies like pink, red, and orange flowers. Moths, which fly at night, like white and cream flowers as they are easier to see.

Nectar guides

Some flowers, like this Alpine eyebright, have patterns on their petals called **nectar guides**. These spots and stripes help to guide the animals, like runway lights guide aeroplanes. The animals follow the guides to find the nectar and pollen in the centre of the flower.

19

Animal pollinators

Insects, such as bees, butterflies, moths, beetles, and flies, are the most important animal pollinators. Some birds and bats also fly between flowers, pollinating them.

This honeybee is carrying pollen stuck to its legs. The bee will spread this pollen as it flies from flower to flower.

When an animal lands on a flower to feed, pollen on the anthers brushes onto the animal's body. When the animal flies off to feed on another flower, the pollen brushes off onto the stigma. The flower is now pollinated.

Special flowers for special animals

Some flowers are specially designed to be pollinated by one type of animal. For example, hibiscus flowers have anthers and stigmas that stick far out of the flower. As a hummingbird sticks its long beak into the flower to drink the nectar, the anthers rub pollen onto its head. When it visits the next flower, the pollen rubs onto the stigma.

Night scents

Some flowers only release their scent at night. This is because they are pollinated by animals that are active at night, for example moths. Often these night scents are very strong, to help animals find the flowers in the dark.

Hibiscus flowers have a special adaptation that means the hummingbird can pollinate them.

Blowing in the wind

Some flowers are pollinated by the wind. The pollen gets blown off and carried in the wind to another flower. These flowers make very light pollen grains that can stay afloat in the air.

Pollen from the flowers on this alder tree is blown by the wind to pollinate other flowers.

Most grasses and trees are pollinated by the wind. Their flowers don't need to be colourful or scented as they don't need to attract animals. Many trees have separate male flowers and female flowers.

Special shapes

Flowers pollinated by the wind usually have long, dangly stamens. This means that the wind can easily blow the pollen off the anthers. They also often have large, feathery stigmas that can catch the pollen blowing about in the air.

Bless you!

Some people are allergic to pollen. When they breathe in the tiny grains carried by the wind, it makes their nose, eyes, and throat become itchy and red. This allergy is called **hay fever**, and it makes some people sneeze their way through the summer.

Flowers become fruits

After a flower has been pollinated, its job is finished. The petals start to shrivel up and die, and eventually they drop off. Meanwhile, the fertilized ovules turn into seeds. Some flowers make only one seed, while others make hundreds. The seeds grow inside the ovaries. As the seeds grow, the ovaries turn into **fruits** around them.

After a flower is pollinated, it doesn't need petals to attract pollinators anymore! The flower may look dead, but seeds are growing inside.

Many kinds of fruit

You can probably think of lots of fruits that have seeds inside them, such as apples, oranges, plums, and cherries. Most of the fruits you can think of are juicy and fleshy.

These seeds are growing inside pods on a tropical chestnut tree.

Fruit or vegetable?

Some things that we think of as vegetables, for example cucumbers, are actually fruits! Anything that contains seeds inside it is a fruit.

However, fruits can also be dry and hard. Acorns and poppy capsules are hard, dry fruits that grow around their seeds. Some fruits are **pods**, such as pea pods. Pods are long, dry fruits that contain rows of seeds.

Flowers around the world

Flowering plants grow almost everywhere on Earth. Some have special features that help them live where conditions are tough. These special features are called adaptations.

This yellow water lily sticks its flower above the surface of the water.

Many plants that grow in water stick their flowers above the surface. This means that they can be pollinated by insects.

Plants in very cold places have small flowers that grow close to the ground. This helps them to stay out of the cold winds. They can flower and make seeds in a very short time while the weather is warm enough.

Flowers such as this *Hydnora abyssinica* give off a terrible, rotten smell. This attracts flies, who then pollinate the flower.

Desert survivor

There is a strange plant that lives in desert areas in Africa. It is called *Hydnora africana*, and most of it lives underground. This protects it from the desert heat. Only the flower emerges above the ground. It needs flies and dung beetles to pollinate it, so it attracts them with its dung-scented flower.

Wonderful weeds

You might think that flowers couldn't grow in towns and cities. But next time you are out, keep a close lookout! You will find little flowers growing all around: in walls, pavement cracks, car parks, and grassy motorway shoulders. These flowers can grow in very little soil.

Flowers and us

We use flowers for lots of different things. We use them for decoration in our homes and for giving to people as presents. We grow them in parks and gardens to add colour and beauty.

Flower shops have a huge range of beautiful flowers to pick from.

We can use the scented oil from sweet-smelling flowers to make perfumes. We can also use the strong colours in flowers to make dye.

Flowers and food

We eat many of the fruits made by flowers. We can also eat some flowers, such as nasturtium flowers. We eat honey, which is made from nectar. We also eat lots of other things that are parts of flowering plants, including rice, wheat, barley, oats, and vegetables. Without flowering plants, we would starve!

Flower meanings

Over the years, some flowers have been given particular meanings. For example, snowdrops mean hope, daffodils stand for new beginnings, and snapdragons mean strength.

Flowers are very special. They can look beautiful, and many ideas for art and design are taken from flowers. Flowers also do a really important job – making seeds to grow into new plants.

Glossary

adaptation feature of a living thing that has changed over time to suit the environment

anther part of the stamen that has pollen on it

bud swelling on a plant that can grow into new parts, such as leaves or a flower

carbon dioxide gas with no colour or smell that is found in the air

carpel female part of a flower where the seeds are made

chlorophyll green substance in plant leaves and stems that traps sunlight for photosynthesis

cross-pollination when pollen from an anther pollinates the stigma of a flower on another plant

fertilization when pollen joins with an ovule to become a seed

fruit part of a plant that surrounds the seeds as they grow

hay fever allergy to pollen. Hay fever makes people have itchy eyes and noses, runny noses, and sneezing fits.

life cycle sequence of changes that a living thing goes through until its death

nectar sweet liquid made by plants to attract animals. When the animals eat the nectar they gather pollen that they can then take to another flower.

nectar guide pattern on a flower that guides animals to where the nectar can be found

nutrient chemical that helps plants to live and grow

ovary part of a flower that contains the ovule

ovule very small female cell in plants that develops into a seed when it is fertilized

photosynthesis process by which plants use water, sunlight, and carbon dioxide to make food for themselves

pod long, thin, firm pouch that contains the seeds of a pea or bean plant

pollen fine powder found on anthers. It is used by plants to fertilize flowers to make seeds.

pollination process by which male plant cells, carried in pollen, land on female parts of the flower

producer living thing that makes food for itself and does not have to eat other things

roots parts of plants that usually grow underground. They take water and nutrients from the soil, and hold the plant in the ground.

self-pollination when pollen from an anther pollinates the stigma of the same flower

sepal part of a plant, shaped like a leaf, that lies at the base of a flower. Sepals hold and protect developing flower buds.

stalk plant part that grows from the stem and supports a leaf or a flower

stamen male part of a flower that includes the anther

stem main part of a plant that supports the branches, leaves, and flowers

stigma female part of a flower where pollen can land and travel to meet the ovule